SUCCEEDING
THE AKSHAY KUMAR WAY

Virender Kapoor is a thinker, an educationist, and an inspirational guru. An alumnus of IIT Bombay and the former director of a prestigious management institute under the Symbiosis umbrella, he also holds a Master's in International Relations and Strategic Studies from Pune University. His books on emotional intelligence, leadership, and self-help have been translated into several regional and foreign languages. A prolific writer, he regularly contributes to *The Times of India*, *The Economic Times*, Rediff.com, and several management magazines. To know more about him, log on to www.virenderkapoor.com or mail him at virenderkapoor21@yahoo.com

Other books in the series:

Speaking: The Modi Way
Leadership: The Gandhi Way
Innovation: The Einstein Way
Excellence: The Amitabh Bachchan Way

SUCCEEDING
THE AKSHAY KUMAR WAY

VIRENDER KAPOOR

Published by
Rupa Publications India Pvt. Ltd 2018
7/16, Ansari Road, Daryaganj
New Delhi 110002

Sales Centres:

Allahabad Bengaluru Chennai
Hyderabad Jaipur Kathmandu
Kolkata Mumbai

Copyright © Virender Kapoor 2018

The views and opinions expressed in this book are the author's own and the facts are as reported by her which have been verified to the extent possible, and the publishers are not in any way liable for the same.

All rights reserved.
No part of this publication may be reproduced, transmitted, or stored in a retrieval system, in any form or by any means, electronic, mechanical, photocopying, recording or otherwise, without the prior permission of the publisher.

ISBN: 978-93-5304-367-4

First impression 2018

10 9 8 7 6 5 4 3 2 1

The moral right of the author has been asserted.

Printed at Parksons Graphics Pvt.Ltd., Mumbai.

This book is sold subject to the condition that it shall not, by way of trade or otherwise, be lent, resold, hired out, or otherwise circulated, without the publisher's prior consent, in any form of binding or cover other than that in which it is published.

CONTENTS

Preface   *vii*

1. Bangkok to Bollywood: A Journey Full of Twists and Turns   1
2. Singh is Kinng: Being Royal and Magnanimous in Deed   14
3. Fit as a Fiddle   30
4. Head in the Clouds and Feet Firmly on the Ground   47
5. Taking Risks, Making Opportunities   61
6. The Ultimate Success Formula: Practice Professionalism   76
7. The Winning Traits: Versatile, Disruptive, and Bankable   89
8. Beyond Professional Success: The Personal Side of Akshay Kumar   100

PREFACE

What is success? Is it money, name, fame, health, family, respect, happiness, professional acclaim, or satisfaction? I feel it is all of it put together. No point in having enormous amounts of money if you are not healthy; no point in being healthy and fit if you have no money; and no point in having professional success, name, and fame if you are not respected.

Therefore, success is like a kaleidoscope, it has multiple layers and colours and patterns. Each time you rotate it, it presents itself differently. Similarly success is also shifty. It is perceived differently at different points in our lives as a journey in time. For instance, you may give more weightage to money when you are young, but you might start leaning more towards fame and professional prowess as you move forward. And even later, your priority may shift to having a stable family life. Yet at all points in time, you need most of these as your 'happiness package'—the contents of this package might keep changing a bit here or there.

Being a film actor is a very tough and challenging profession. Firstly, the shelf life of a mainstream actor is usually limited to a few years. Secondly, success is difficult if not illusive and when it comes, it comes in a flash and also disappears in a blink. Thirdly, this profession is very demanding in terms of rigorous chaotic schedules which can take a toll on family life, health, and one's overall well-being.

When I thought of writing a book on Akshay Kumar, I had to be convinced myself that this man is in fact successful; in the terms of what I consider to be success. There are so many successful actors in Indian cinema who have earned a name, enough fame, pots of money and are appreciated as great performers by the audience. Then, why should I write about Akshay?

As I researched further, I realized that he is a perfect role model for the youth and also for the elderly. Clean as a whistle, devoid of major controversies, gentlemanly, and above all perceived as a person far removed from arrogance—very grounded and humble. And he is a successful box office hero, who is loved by his audience and his directors in equal measure. He is a bankable star who has delivered very versatile performances. He may not be compared to greats such as Al Pacino, Marlon Brando, Morgan Freeman, Robert De Niro, Tom Hanks, Mel Gibson, or a Dustin Hoffman, in terms of their brilliant acting prowess recognized by the jury at the Oscars—but he is a box office phenomenon in India who sells, and sells very well.

Akshay Kumar has never boasted about his acting skills, though from time to time he has done films where he has shown his prowess. On the awards front, he may not have bagged as many awards and nominations as his contemporaries like Shah Rukh Khan and Aamir Khan have, but his record is quite respectable with a total of 13 wins and 29 nominations, two of which were Filmfare Awards.[1] He has enjoyed a fair share of critical acclaim for his work in films like *Sangharsh*, *Hera Pheri*, *Dhadkan*, *Khakee*, *Bhagam Bhag*, *Namastey London*, *8x10 Tasveer*, *Special 26*, *Baby*, *Airlift*, and *Rustom*. He also bagged the National Award for Best Actor in *Rustom* and *Airlift*, two Filmfare Awards for Best Comedian (*Garam Masala*, 2005) and Best Villain (*Ajnabee*, 2001) respectively. He also picked up a few awards at IIFA, Stardust, Screen, BIG Star Entertainment, Zee Cine Awards, etc. Not to miss his Dadasaheb Phalke Awards, bestowed upon him by the Dadasaheb Phalke Film Foundation for his films *Rowdy Rathore* (2013), *Toilet: Ek Prem Katha*, and *Pad Man* (2018).

He is no lesser than any other Indian cinema hero.

---

[1] Source: IMDb

He stands first amongst equals as far as his popularity and saleability is concerned.

Cut to his other humanly traits which far outweigh any actor's professional prowess, crowd-pulling strength, or any blockbuster film—are what makes him stand head and shoulders above his contemporaries.

He is a family man, a fitness freak, daredevil, and a man who lives by his own definition of life. He doesn't believe in 'work hard and party harder' philosophy. He has a conservative lifestyle, neither ostentatiously extravagant nor highly extravagant…and yet stylish and a cut above others. He is very careful about his diet and is regular with exercise. He works hard to complete his movies on time and many a times, aims to finish before the time frame which the producer has in mind, simply because he believes that completing a movie on time will reduce the production cost and help the producer earn his return on investment. It is smart thinking, but most actors don't think this way. He also does charity in different ways, like supporting the Indian Army.

What more does one look for in a man? Akshay Kumar is truly a model of success, and an inspiration for youngsters to learn from through this book.

1

BANGKOK TO BOLLYWOOD
A Journey Full of Twists and Turns

'Twenty years from now you will be more disappointed by the things that you didn't do than by the ones you did do. So throw off the bowlines. Sail away from the safe harbour. Catch the trade winds in your sails. Explore. Dream. Discover.'

—Mark Twain

Born as Rajiv Hari Om Bhatia, Akshay Kumar's is a typical rags-to-riches story. A boy born in a middle-class Punjabi family in Amritsar, whose father was a soldier in the Indian Army, and who had very little to celebrate as such, materialistically speaking—went on to become one of the richest actors in the Indian film industry. His father

Hari Om Bhatia later changed his profession and worked as an accountant in UNICEF, Delhi. Akshay grew up in Chandni Chowk, the very crowded part of Old Delhi. Eventually, the family shifted to Mumbai and lived in Koliwada—yet another lower middle-class area populated by mostly Punjabi families. His father brought him up with army discipline—waking up by 5 a.m. every day, going for a jog and exercising were part of his daily routine. He acquired these good habits at a very young age because of his father. Rituals like early to bed and early to rise became a lifestyle for Akshay, which he still sticks to.

He was lucky to have studied at Don Bosco School—his caring middle-class parents' vision and willingness to spend money on his education. There's an interesting story behind how he got admission in the school, which was no easy feat. When he went for the school interview with his father, he saw a piece of paper lying on the ground. He picked it up and put it in the dustbin. The principal of the school saw that and was so impressed by the gesture that he gave him admission without an interview!

★

Akshay was neither good at nor interested in studies and

instead preferred to spend more time on outdoor games. He was terribly reprimanded by his father for poor marks in his Class Seven exams. Later, realizing that he had little interest in academics, his father eventually stopped pushing him for studies and began encouraging him to learn martial arts. Hence, Akshay began practicing Taekwondo and achieved a black belt in it while still in India. He had joined Guru Nanak Khalsa College in Mumbai, but dropped out in a year to proceed to Bangkok, Thailand to learn more in martial arts.

Learn to Earn

Akshay Kumar is a rich and a mighty star today. But behind this success is the story of his struggles and learning to earn a living. While training in Bangkok for martial arts, he worked as a waiter in hotels to support himself, and also did a few more odd jobs. He would even sell jewellery to get himself some money. After returning from Bangkok, where he had learned the combat sport, Muay Thai, he started his own martial art training classes.

In my MBA institute, we used to have an interesting exercise for the fresh batches. It was called 'earn a day's living'. After a couple of weeks when the students had settled down into the course's rhythm, one fine morning it was announced that the students need to earn their living for a day. Their wallets were taken in custody and they were told to go to the market and pick up a job for eight hours and see how much could they earn. They could do any job as long as they did not reveal to their employer that they were students of a prestigious management institute.

It was a shocker for them to fend for themselves for the day. Since they didn't have money for even bus fare, some walked, while some managed to get a lift. They would take up all sorts of jobs—from washing utensils, becoming a sales man, or even polishing shoes for people. These were jobs they had never done before. Some students had rich parents and they had been terribly pampered, for them this would be an experience of a lifetime. By the time they would return back to the campus it would be late in the evening. Some would have made good money and some very little. But everyone would be happy that they had made their own money. Most would want to frame the currency notes and retain those as a souvenir!

Start of a Great Journey: His Modelling Stint

Akshay was told by one of his students that he was smart

and good-looking, and should try his luck in modelling and even films. He met the photographer Jayesh Sheth and asked him to shoot his modelling portfolio. Jayesh clicked him in some stunt poses and those came out rather well. Thanks to the shots, Akshay was beginning to get a few modelling assignments. He realized that from it he could make more money in two days than what he made in a month by teaching martial arts. In order to pay Jayesh for the shoot, Akshay worked as his assistant for free for eighteen months; meanwhile, also working as a background dancer in films.

Thereafter, he started taking modelling seriously and tried getting more assignments. It so happened once that there was an important assignment for which he had to travel to Bengaluru. Unfortunately, he missed his flight and lost that opportunity. He was reprimanded and told that he would never be able to become a successful model with such carelessness. Anyone can miss a flight, but when you are a nobody and struggling to make a career, even one mistake can be magnified by the powers that be.

He was quite disgusted and thought of trying his luck in films instead. Most aspiring actors come from outside Mumbai and face two challenges—to find a place to live in the city and to find work. In Akshay's case, he was already living in Mumbai and that was his saving grace.

The Transformation: From Rajiv Bhatia to Akshay Kumar

Akshay's film journey started with almost an insignificant role. His first film, where he had just a 4.5-second long role was *Aaj* (1987) directed by Mahesh Bhatt. This film had actor Kumar Gaurav in the lead role and his character's name was 'Akshay'. Having been inspired by Gaurav and his acting, Rajiv Bhatia went ahead and changed his name to Akshay at a court in Mumbai.[1]

I feel Rajiv Bhatia is as good a name as Rajesh Khanna, Vinod Khanna, or Sidharth Malhotra or anybody else, but many people who enter the show business do change their name for some reason or the other. It turned out for the better; Akshay Kumar suited him and possibly changed his destiny.

His first lead role in a film was in *Saugandh* (1991) directed by Raj Sippy and starring Rakhee and Shantipriya. But his first major film was Abbas Mastaan's *Khiladi* in 1992, with which his success journey began. The same year, he appeared in the Pramod Chakravorty-produced film, *Deedar*.

---

[1] https://www.indiatoday.in/movies/bollywood/story/akshay-kumar-first-pay-cheque-name-change-jo-jeeta-wohi-sikander-1095003-2017-11-27

In 1994, Kumar earned his first nomination for Best Actor at the Filmfare Awards for his performance in the Yash Chopra-produced *Yeh Dillagi*. That same year he starred in Rajiv Rai's *Mohra* as well, which went on to be a big success at the box office.

Akshay's 'Khiladi' tag became a runaway hit, and Bollywood developed a popular franchise off it and made eight films under it, with the last one being *Khiladi 786* in 2012. The other films in the Khiladi series include: *Main Khiladi Tu Anari* (1994), *Sabse Bada Khiladi* (1995), *Khiladiyon Ka Khiladi* (1996), *Mr. and Mrs. Khiladi* (1997), *International Khiladi* (1999), and *Khiladi 420* (2000). There has been no looking back for him since, and he remains to this day one of the most sought-after actors in Bollywood.

It is worth noting that this man had no godfather nor did he have any relation in the industry. Everything he has achieved has been with his sheer hard work, talent, and professionalism.

His success can be measured by this example: If you leap and lunge from a height of ninety feet and reach a target of hundred feet, your jump is of primarily only ten feet. But if you lunge from ten feet and reach a target of hundred, you have jumped ninety feet. Akshay lunged the full ninety feet as his take-off was almost from the ground level because he had no one to launch him or promote him initially.

Journey through Thick and Thin

Filmy roller-coaster takes you to dizzying heights and also through certain dips which can be mind-shattering. For such a career to bloom and flourish, one needs to have a lot of patience and a never-say-die attitude all the time. It's a long road, and along the way you come across success, failures, applause, and even humiliation in equal measures.

In a career spanning over twenty-five years, Akshay has had his share of bouquets and brickbats that one gets while rising in the tinsel town. After a successful string of films like *Khiladi* and *Mohra*, several of his other releases in the 1990s, including *Lahoo Ke Do Rang, Insaaf, Daava, Tarazu, Angaaray, Barood,* and *Zulmi*, performed poorly at the box office, leading to a setback in his film career.

In the year 2000, he starred in the Priyadarshan-directed comedy, *Hera Pheri*, which helped him prove his excellent comic timing in the film. It did very well at the box office, and helped him bounce back from his string of flops. The film also helped him explore beyond his 'action hero' tag, which by then was established firmly because of his ever-appealing macho persona and daredevil stunts. In 2001 came *Ajnabee*, in which Akshay played a negative role—a performance that won him the Filmfare Award for the Best Villain. He had by then become an established star and a much-appreciated actor.

In 2004, he starred in a romantic thriller called *Aitraaz*, delivering a brilliant performance as a married man who is wrongfully accused of sexual harassment by his employer's wife, a negative role that was essayed quite well by Priyanka Chopra. Next, he appeared in David Dhawan's romantic comedy *Mujhse Shaadi Karogi* in the same year. In 2004 itself, he presented the television series *Seven Deadly Arts with Akshay Kumar* on National Geographic Channel. He also received a nomination for the Filmfare Award for Best Supporting Actor for his role in the multi-starrer action thriller *Khakee* the same year.

The following years gave him an opportunity to move up by several notches in his career. *Garam Masala* earned him that Filmfare Award in 2006. In the next few years, Kumar starred in four consecutive commercially successful films; the romantic comedy *Welcome*, psychological thriller *Bhool Bhulaiyaa*, and the comedies *Heyy Babyy* and *Namastey London*.

By the middle of that decade Akshay Kumar was on a roll.

In 2008, he founded Hari Om Entertainment Co. and also hosted the first season of the reality game show, *Fear Factor: Khatron Ke Khiladi* which was a great hit with the audience. The following year he was awarded the Padma Shri Award for his contribution to cinema.

He went on to produce the Indo-Canadian hockey-based film *Breakaway*, which became the highest grossing cross-cultural film at the Canadian box office. His next two films *Rowdy Rathore* and *Housefull 2* grossed over ₹100 crore each at the box office. For him, 2013 was a year of dramas and thrillers. *Special 26* was very well appreciated by all and the crime drama *Once Upon a Time in Mumbai Dobaara!*, although not appreciated much, did well commercially.

In 2015, Akshay earned a nomination for the Filmfare Best Actor Award for his performance in the comic-drama *Singh Is Kinng*, again a comedy film with a message.

He has always demonstrated a patriotic inclination with films like *Namastey London*, *Baby*, *Airlift*, *Rustom*, among others. Playing an Indian espionage agent in *Baby*, Akshay again showed his awe-inspiring stunts and used his fitness to the hilt for this role. In *Rustom*, he gave a brilliant performance playing the role of an Indian naval officer and carried it off very convincingly. To play a character and look like it are two different things. In *Rustom*, he mastered the appearance of a serving naval officer; he got the mannerism, grace, and chivalrous attitude right for the film—leading to the National Film Award for Best Actor for his performance, which he fully deserved.

For him, 2017 was also a great year of celebration and success. His movies *Jolly LL.B 2*, *Naam Shabana*, and *Toilet: Ek Prem Katha* were all exceptionally good movies.

Toilet: Ek Prem Katha was made with the purpose of discouraging the issue of open defecation across India and was in sync with Prime Minister Narendra Modi's 'Swachh Bharat Abhiyan'. Commercially speaking, he gave his producers an extremely lucky run in 2015, 2016, and 2017, as most of his movies grossed over ₹100 crore in revenue just domestically.

Akshay never stops experimenting. One of his most recent films is *Pad Man*, the idea for which came from his wife. It was made to spread awareness about female menstrual hygiene and the use of sanitary napkins, mostly in rural India. It was a risky subject to begin with, considering the Indian audience. But it was made with care, and the film received success at the box office too. Akshay has now reached a stage in his career where he can afford to experiment; and this is the greatest lesson for all of us—when you reach the top and are financially secured, do give back to the society as much as you can through your own medium.

> 'I've missed more than 9,000 shots in my career. I've lost almost 300 games. Twenty-six times, I've been trusted to take the game winning shot and missed. I've failed over and over and over again in my life. And that is why I succeed.'
>
> —*Michael Jordan*

What can you learn from Akshay Kumar to live your life to the fullest?

1. Follow your heart, do what you like and go with the flow—success will certainly follow you. He began with martial arts and moved on to modelling and then to cinema, always following his instinct.
2. Be good and people will be good to you. His school principal noticed him picking up a waste paper from the ground and putting it into a dustbin and for that good deed he got admission in a good school.
3. Bring up your children with good values so that they grow into good people and good citizens.
4. Your children must learn to earn their success. Nothing

should be given to them on a platter. This is the biggest mistake most parents in India make when they unduly pamper and protect children who are later unable to face the world on their own.
5. Once you are married, remain committed to your spouse. The strength of a couple is togetherness and mutual support through thick and thin. Share your problems with each other and the load gets divided. If both have their heart in place, then the equation changes. One plus one is not two but eleven—'*Ek aur ek gyarah*'.
6. Learn to take success and failure in your stride. Promotion, success, and failure are all a part of life. Even in Akshay's career, there were some super hit films, some average performers, and many flops too. To bash on regardless should be your mantra. It's the law of averages that makes for such balances in life.

2

SINGH IS KINNG
Being Royal and Magnanimous in Deed

*'A lion is called a "king of beasts"
obviously for a reason.'*

—Jack Hanna

The media in India has been known to attach tags to top Bollywood stars, typecasting them in the process. We are all familiar with Amitabh Bachchan being referred to as 'Shahenshah', Shah Rukh Khan as 'King Khan' or 'Badshah of Bollywood', and Salman Khan labelled as 'Sultan', etc. While these may be good for the ego of the actors, but more often than not these are a bit over the top and sound pretty haughty. Fortunately, for the more recent stream of actors like Ranbir Kapoor,

Ranveer Singh, Hrithik Roshan, and many others who have made their mark in the industry, have not been tagged with a title as of yet; but perhaps they too will be, after a while.

Akshay Kumar has been working resolutely and chugging along at a steady pace since the 1990s, which makes him a kind of veteran with close to three decades of work under his belt. He too was tagged as 'Khiladi Kumar', all thanks to his several films with 'Khiladi' as the title!

Although not touted as Bollywood royalty, but he is a king—a person who possesses traits of a *'zinda dil raja'* (large-hearted king). He has done plenty over the years and that too splendidly, with a fair share of hits and misses, bagging awards on the way, and making enough money for his producers and for himself.

In addition to being a highly successful and a bankable actor who can carry a film entirely on his shoulders, Akshay Kumar has certain traits which many of the top stars of Hindi cinema do not possess. Very humane and down to earth, he is a man liked by everyone in the show business. And that is why he always has the support of the entire industry when required. When Hrithik Roshan's *Mohenjo Daro* and Akshay's *Rustom* clashed at the box office by releasing on the same date, the two superstars supported each other in a rare camaraderie.

Hrithik was the first to tweet saying '#MohenjoDaro is just 4 days away. And so is #Rustom (wink)'. Akshay reciprocated by saying '...get ready with your popcorn guys, entertaining weekend ahead.'[2] Getting support and respect within your own fraternity is the biggest achievement. So much so that even producers listen to his suggestions with an open mind.

'The whole difference between construction and creation is exactly this: that a thing constructed can only be loved after it is constructed; but a thing created is loved before it exists.'

—*Charles Dickens*

Akshay Is a Real King

According to Chanakya, a scholar and Emperor Chandragupta Maurya's mentor, a king must possesses certain qualities. Some of the most relevant ones are:

---

[2]https://indianexpress.com/article/entertainment/bollywood/hrithik-roshan-supports-akshay-kumar-and-ends-rustom-vs-mohenjo-daro-debate-like-a-boss-2962158/

1. Royalty has a charm, and with poise and confidence the royals command respect.
2. They are dignified and sophisticated.
3. Kings are neither dilatory, nor do they delay things. If there is a problem they attend to it immediately.
4. They are full of gratitude.
5. They must have self-control.
6. Great kings are amenable to guidance and mentoring.
7. They keep their promise.
8. They are large-hearted.

In his professional and personal life, Akshay Kumar has somewhat similar qualities like that of a king:

1. He is known to be accepting of his mistakes and is always quick to apologize.
2. Once his bodyguard punched a fan who wanted a selfie with Akshay, but he was quick to give an official apology and declare that such a thing would never happen again.
3. He is an extremely disciplined man and demonstrates great self-control. The reason his films do well financially is because he delivers his best in time. He works hard to ensure that a film is made in the shortest possible time.
4. Akshay seldom loses temper and is always measured in his response.

5. He maintains a clean image and he has not been embroiled in any major controversy in a career spanning three decades. He never speaks ill about any of his co-stars or directors.
6. He is bold enough to make off-beat choices and do films on socially relevant subjects. This is evident through some of his recent films like *Jolly LL.B 2* (a satire on judiciary); *Toilet: Ek Prem Katha* (on the issue of open defecation); and *Pad Man* (on the importance of menstrual hygiene).

Large-Hearted: *'Zinda Dil'*

There is no particular reason for as to why some people are large-hearted and do a lot of charity, while others don't. Plenty of people in this world have enough that they can spare a bit of it for the lesser privileged ones, but not everyone does that. But, there are still some good people who are helpful and give back to the society. Mostly, this is very individualistic and a matter of personal choice. Some people learn this by observing the world and develop sensitivity towards the needy over a period of time. And others may have survived through difficult times in childhood and wish to help others when they have enough because they can relate to their anguish.

Akshay Kumar comes from an extremely humble

background; he has seen what it is like to live with limited means in a small house where he lived with his parents and sister. He understands where the shoe pinches and is ready to help those who need it. He also didn't get anything on the platter and had to struggle to make ends meet. He knows the value of money and the pain of failure and rejection.

He is always helpful towards people who work with him or for him. He donates generously and is among the most charitable actors from Bollywood, along with Aamir Khan, Sonam Kapoor, and Shabana Azmi.[3]

Akshay had said during the promotions of his film *Rustom* that he wanted to serve the nation by joining the army, but destiny had something else for him. His heart goes out to those in the armed forces, who sacrifice their youth and sometimes even life for the nation. He now lives his dream by choosing films with patriotic themes. He has played a soldier in *Holiday: A Soldier Is Never Off Duty*, a special agent in *Baby*, and a naval officer in *Rustom*, he will play a British

---

[3] http://www.mtvindia.com/blogs/news/play/7-most-charitable-bollywood-celebrities-52197337.html

soldier in his upcoming film, *Kesari*.

Although Akshay hasn't talked much about his charity acts, one can find out about some of it with a little bit of research. In 2016, he donated ₹90 lakh to help the drought-hit farmers in Maharashtra. The same year Akshay also donated ₹80 lakh to the families of army men, saying our soldiers need money along with 'samman'.

He donated more than ₹1 crore to the martyred jawans of CRPF who were killed in Chhattisgarh. Apart from providing monetary help, he also visited the BSF base camp in Jammu to pay tribute to soldiers who have lost their lives in ceasefire violations. During his visit, an emotional Kumar called them the 'real heroes'. He said, 'I am fortunate that I got the opportunity to come and meet you. I have always said I'm a reel hero, you are the real hero.'[4]

Not just the army, Akshay has come forward to help other causes as well. In December 2015 when Chennai was hit by massive floods, he came forward to help and donated a whopping ₹1 crore to a trust helping with Chennai floods relief work.[5]

---

[4]http://www.tribuneindia.com/news/jammu-kashmir/community/bsf-jawans-real-heroes-akshay-kumar/320450.html

[5]https://www.indiatimes.com/entertainment/celebs/7-times-akshay-kumar-proved-that-he-is-the-most-humble-grounded-bollywood-actor-256888.html

In *Khataron Ke Khiladi*, when one participant was eliminated from the show due to non-performance, Akshay asked him, 'What would you have done if you had won the prize money of ₹25 lakh?' The participant replied that he would have used the money for his father's treatment as he was suffering from cancer. Akshay generously gave him a cheque of the same amount from his own account.

To provide free self-defence training to women in Mumbai, Akshay Kumar has launched a martial arts school where almost 4,000 women have already been trained! In another example of his magnanimity, Akshay donated all proceeds of a Punjabi devotional song, 'Nirgun Raakh Liya' which he sang and featured in its video, to the victims of the train bombings of Mumbai on 11 July 2006. He even supports his fellow actors in their charitable initiatives: for example he donated ₹50 lakh to Salman Khan's charity organization, Being Human.[6]

---

[6]Instances referred from https://indianexpress.com/article/entertainment/bollywood/akshay-kumar-donates-rs-1-08-cr-to-martyred-jawans-9-times-he-helped-people-in-need-4573062/ and https://www.indiatimes.com/entertainment/celebs/7-times-akshay-kumar-proved-that-he-is-the-most-humble-grounded-bollywood-actor-256888.html

Motivating Others to Do Good Deeds

Doing things yourself is good, but when you have a celebrity's status you can do much more than that by involving others for a cause. While Akshay does charity himself, he also motivates others to do the same. Realizing that many people wanted to donate money for the soldiers who defend our country, Akshay took the initiative to create a system where people could easily donate money to help nation's defenders. The result is 'Bharat Ke Veer', an app with the help of Government of India, which provided a transparent system to extend some monetary help for Indian soldiers.

That's not all. To promote sports and athletics he has urged the corporates to support those who have talent but come from underprivileged backgrounds and have no money to spend on sports. He says, 'Cricket... I am just damn tired of it! I want something else coming out of this country. I just want it to happen. Support these families, their children are made of something which can get us gold medals at Olympics.'[7]

---

[7]https://www.firstpost.com/entertainment/akshay-kumar-urges-corporates-to-support-budding-sports-talent-629715.html

Gestures Demonstrate the Intent

More than actions, it is your intention that matters. This demonstrates your psyche and bent of mind. Akshay's intent to help people and his patriotism towards his country also reflects in the kind of films he chooses to do. And hence he has played the role of a man in uniform quite a few times, *Rustom* and *Holiday* being the most popular examples. Films with a message have also been a way for him to promote certain ideas.

With *Toilet: Ek Prem Katha*, he brought forth the issue of open defecation and with *Pad Man* the problems of menstrual hygiene faced by women in rural India due to either the unavailability of sanitary napkins or because of its expense. The latter was a story identified by Akshay's wife, Twinkle Khanna, and the film was directed by R. Balki. Again, a risky subject from the box office point of view; one has seen iconic characters like Batman, Spiderman, etc. but had you ever imagined a Pad Man? It was based on the real-life story of Arunachalam Muruganantham, the original Pad Man. A school dropout, he was moved after noticing his wife using unhygienic rags during menstruation. He made several types of pads and asked his sister and wife to try them, which initially didn't work. He kept working on making it better till he found the right material. Today, he is known all over the world for having created machines that produce low-cost sanitary napkins that are sold in India as well as abroad. He now rubs shoulders with the likes of Bill Gates and James Cameron, when he gives lectures at IITs, IIMs, and Harvard University. In 2016, *Time* magazine featured him as one of the 100 Most Influential People in the world.[8]

A good man looks at others also as good people. If your own feelings are pure and not filled with treacherous ideas, you will also look at others in the same way. Once during a thunderstorm and heavy rainfall in Mumbai, a man intruded into Akshay's house looking for shelter after managing to escape the security guard's notice. Later, he was caught and handed over to the police. When Akshay came to know of the matter he called the police station to know what had actually happened. He was told that the man had rushed into his house only to save himself from the downpour and had no intention of stealing anything. Akshay then requested the police to release him.[9]

---

[8]https://yourstory.com/2016/03/arunachalam-muruganantham-time-magazine/
[9]https://www.timesnownews.com/entertainment/news/bollywood-news/article/akshay-kumar-is-a-large-hearted-soul/147116

Helping within the Fraternity

Film industry is known to be a very cold-hearted place where people care only for those who are successful and who can help you in moving up the ladder. People can be calculative and, to a large extent, self-centred who can stoop to any level before the people who matter. It could be directors, producers, and established stars. They get referred to as godfathers. This stands true for even Hollywood. Unfortunately, junior artistes, earlier called 'extras' (a derogatory word), are not given any space or even dignity within the film industry. Stuntmen and stuntwomen take all the risks by performing dangerous stunts, but in return they are neither paid well nor looked after if the stunts go wrong and they get injured.

In March 2016, Akshay Kumar had penned down a heartfelt letter to all the stuntmen and stuntwomen of Bollywood. In his open letter, he didn't just thank them but also proposed how they deserve much more than the wage package. An excerpt of his letter reads:

> You deserve so much more than just a wage packet, and I hope I live long enough to see a change in that. I know that in my 25-year-long career nothing much has changed! But it will, and I will try and make sure

of that... Till then thank you and take great care. Good luck with the fight for your rights... RIP to all those who have lost their lives.[10]

Akshay has time and again emphasized on how he is first a stuntman and then an actor. His views have always been candid; he strongly feels for the stuntmen and how their passion towards their craft deserves a lot more validation, recognition, and monetary benefits. He has started an insurance scheme for the stuntmen and stuntwomen of Bollywood. The scheme is going to cover 380 stuntmen and women between 18–55 years of age. In case of hospitalization due to any physical injury or accident while doing stunts, a stuntman will be covered for ₹6 lakh at about 4,000 hospitals through a cashless system. In case of death, a sum of ₹10 lakh will be given to the nominee.[11]

Hindi film industry is almost a hundred years old now, yet it took one Akshay Kumar to do this. Not that it could not have been done by anyone else, but as I said gestures

---

[10] https://www.hindustantimes.com/bollywood/akshay-kumar-pens-open-letter-to-stuntmen-i-m-alive-thanks-to-you/story-x6qgBRcWcwhUH6AWTHPgOL.html

[11] https://www.indiatimes.com/entertainment/celebs/akshay-kumar-s-visionary-idea-comes-to-life-insurance-scheme-for-stuntmen-stuntwomen-launched-276289.html

matter and your intentions should be to do something good for others.

'The results of philanthropy are
always beyond calculation.'

—*Mary Ritter Beard*

In the beginning of 2018, Akshay's *Pad Man* and Sanjay Leela Bhansali's *Padmaavat* were ready to clash upon their release. But Akshay delayed the release of *Pad Man* to 9 February to give *Padmaavat* a full one-week free run. *Padmaavat* had earlier been delayed due to violent protests against it by a particular community. Not only Bhansali, but the entire team of *Padmaavat* thanked him for his kind gesture.

Actress Deepika Padukone, who played the title role in the film, expressed her gratitude to Akshay by sending him a note: 'On behalf of team *Padmaavat*, a big, big thank you to the team *Pad Man* for your support and generosity!' Ranveer Singh tweeted: 'Big man with a big heart! Akshay Kumar, grateful to you sir, much love and respect.' Shahid Kapoor too tweeted his thanks: 'Thank you, Akshay Kumar, for being ever so gracious. Can't wait to see *Pad Man*. Much love and luck.' Respecting the gesture, Bhansali said, 'I will be grateful to Akshay for a lifetime.'[12]

What can you learn from Akshay Kumar about living life king size?

1. Creativity is largely about instinct and gut feeling. Akshay came up with the idea for the film *Singh is Kinng* after seeing 'Singh is King' written at the back of a truck. He immediately took a chance with a producer to make a movie around that title, which happened at the spur of the moment. It says a lot about his creative and business bent of mind.
2. Being large-hearted and forgiving like a great king. Whatever position you are in professionally, there is always a room to demonstrate a royal attitude. And it doesn't happen by being a snob, but by being more royal-like in every situation.
3. Help your colleagues irrespective of their position or hierarchy in the industry, and they will stand by you every

---

[12] https://www.newsx.com/entertainment/i-will-be-grateful-to-akshay-kumar-for-a-lifetime-padmaavat-director-sanjay-leela-bhansali-on-padmans-postponed-release

time you need them. Those within your fraternity who are not as well placed as you are, must be supported by you. Akshay's life insurance cover idea for the stuntmen who take great risks for playing double to the actors and put their life and limbs in danger is an example of just that.
4. Be prepared to take risks and experiment. He did some off-beat cinema which was relevant for the times. He took on risky subjects for mainstream cinema, but was successful with them.
5. Do charity and prod others to help the society. Akshay has been associated with charity work on several occasions.

3

FIT AS A FIDDLE

*'Take care of your body.
It's the only place you have to live.'*

—Jim Rohn

Distractions Aplenty

There are so many distractions, attractions, and opportunities to indulge in whatever way one wants to in the affluent circle of the rich and the famous—especially when you are a star. People are prepared to pamper you, invite you to parties and junkets, they stand in queues to meet you—literally sucking up to your success. Many can't handle this success and hit the bottle, some get on to drugs, and smoking is always in fashion—anytime anywhere.

Staying away from all such addictions requires a very

strong will and desire. People say, 'Yaar, make hay while the sun shines…*aisa mauka phir kahan milega*,' and the answer almost always is 'why not?' This is how people look at success and get into one of the addictions which are not easy to quit. It is with the first drag of a cigarette or hashish, a few parties with alcohol flowing like river…where one becomes a part of the flow, enough to get one hooked to such things.

To remain sane and fit in such an industry is a challenge. At the same time staying fit, maintaining your body and keeping your face looking fresh and shiny is an occupational requirement for every actor. With the exception of Amitabh Bachchan probably, who is still going strong at the age of seventy-five and still has roles pouring in for him, almost all actors need to maintain their looks to keep looking young and fighting fit. Although Bachchan too due to his health issues keeps a strict watch on his diet and does routine exercises appropriate for him.

Following a Health Routine

The challenge of following a routine in a chaotic profession like a film actor's is again a professional hazard. Odd hours, frequent travels, multiple movies being done at the same time always disrupt your routine. A regular person would say 'to hell with it, let me live my life to the fullest' and this is a booby trap, a cardinal sin for any actor, which can finish him or her forever in a profession like this one, where you are paid to look good, if not ravishingly beautiful, then at least fit.

To follow a routine in a structured job which is by and large organized as far as timings are concerned, carving out a routine within that tight routine itself is somewhat simpler. Therefore, any actor who follows his routine within this unstructured profession which is as emotionally demanding as it is physically, is worth admiring.

Akshay Kumar is one such person who can be seen as a role model for following a certain diet and making sincere efforts with a reasonable degree of success to follow a routine which is required to remain healthy and fit. The takeaway for each one of us is that if he can do it despite being a part of such an industry, then why not people in routine jobs?

He is by far the fittest actor in the Indian film industry. There is a prize to be paid for that achievement and it takes all of one's willpower to maintain that position. Most people follow a diet or a routine usually for short periods of time and even that can be a daunting task for them. But to make a disciplined diet part of the lifestyle requires a different mindset.

I feel fitness is more to do with your self-control than anything else. If you want lifetime fitness as a lifestyle, a firm control on your will is essential. You can never let your guard down ever. Like I said earlier, a single drag from a cigarette can destroy everything as it often leads to addiction.

His Fitness Mantras

In an interview given to Rediff.com[13] when Akshay turned fifty, he said, 'I have only one job in my life, and that is to make films.' He also added, 'All I have to do is take care of my family and workout. I avoid getting stressed, and hold onto happiness. There is no science to this. All you have to do is try to live a simple life.' He also said, 'You can always find one hour in a day to look after your health.'

1. **A Good Night's Sleep Is on the Top of the Stack: A Critical Look**
    This is one thing which people don't understand the importance of, especially the young generation. Getting sleep for seven to eight hours and in sync with the natural

---

[13]http://www.rediff.com/getahead/report/health-akshay-kumar-fitness-routine-exercise-how-to-be-fit-at-30-40-and-50/20170909.htm

body clock is the most important practice for a healthy body and sound mind. If you sleep at 3 a.m. and get up at 11 a.m. thinking that you have completed the requisite quota of the day, i.e. 8 hours—then it is not enough; you have committed a cardinal sin by flouting the nature's timings. For instance, birds across the world get up in the morning before sunrise or, say, early morning. It could be China, Japan, or the United States; birds everywhere wake up early morning. They return after a day's work and settle down in their nests before the sun sets and go off to sleep. This way they follow the nature's cycle which keeps them healthy. We, as humans, are a part of the same ecosystem and, therefore, need to follow the same rules. If you look at people working in night shifts, be it a factory or a call centre, there are severe and several cases of people as young as thirty who are falling sick early.

And now there is even published research to prove this point. The Nobel Prize for Medicine in 2017 was awarded to three scientists—Jeffrey C. Hall, Michael Rosbash, and Michael W. Young—for their discoveries of molecular mechanism controlling our internal biological clock. These twenty-four-hour rhythms are driven by a Circadian Clock, and they have been widely observed in plants, animals, fungi, and cyanobacteria. Their discoveries explain 'how plants, animals, and humans adapt their biological rhythm so that it is synchronized with the Earth's revolutions.'

When there is a mismatch between this internal 'clock' and the external surroundings, it can affect the organism's well-being—for example, in humans, it happens when we experience jet lag. Our biological clock helps to regulate sleep patterns, feeding behaviour, hormone release, and blood pressure.

Sir Paul Nurse, who shared the Nobel Prize in 2001 for research on the cell cycle, had said that every living organism on this planet responds to the sun. 'All plant and animal behaviour is determined by the light-dark cycle. We on this planet are slaves to the sun. The circadian clock is embedded in our mechanisms of working, our metabolism, it's embedded everywhere…,' he had said.[14]

Akshay Kumar is no scientist but follows what our grandmothers have been telling us for ages—'early to bed and early to rise'. Unfortunately it is only scientific evidence that convinces many of us now, though our earlier generations learnt it over a period of time and

---

[14]https://www.theguardian.com/science/2017/oct/02/nobel-prize-for-medicine-awarded-for-insights-into-internal-biological-clock

followed these principles which got tried and tested for centuries. They followed their common sense like animals and birds do. They didn't have a scientific evidence yet they practiced it over a long period of time to keep themselves healthy—till our modern generation started questioning and doubting our basic traditions. To prove the point that common sense is the most important trait of a person, Lido Anthony 'Lee' Iacocca, a legendary American automobile executive, had said: 'If it looks like a duck and quacks like a duck, then it probably is a duck!' Akshay Kumar's day starts at 5.30 in the morning and he takes his dinner early at around 7 p.m. and goes to bed by 9 in the night. A little change in the lifestyle can last and help sort out the most difficult challenges that we face as far health is concerned. 'I love my sleep and I love to see the mornings. People who invite me to a party know that I will leave early because I have to be in bed,' he revealed to Karan Johar in one of the episodes of *Koffee with Karan*.[15]

---

[15]https://food.ndtv.com/health/akshay-kumar-turns-49-heres-his-diet-and-formula-for-the-fit-life-1436862

'Sleep is that golden chain that ties health and our bodies together.'

—*Thomas Dekker*

2. You Don't Need a Gym to Remain Fit

Defence personnel across the world, whether from the Indian Army or the US Navy or the British SAS, do not have bulging biceps or six-pack abs and yet it does not define their fitness. They believe in 'functional fitness' which lets you perform your job effectively and makes you feel fit, be fit, and look fit. This is also what all the martial art forms focus on. To do your job effectively and even do stunts, an actor need not look like a Mr Universe.

Akshay Kumar sincerely follows this belief. He has never resorted to any shortcuts to build his body, like taking supplements, powders, or shakes. In order to maintain physical fitness, it's best to build your body naturally.

Fitness comes from keeping your body active and there are different ways to do so without hitting the gym. He is heavily into kick-boxing and shadow-boxing. He also practices parkour (the activity or sport of moving rapidly through an area, typically in an urban environment, negotiating obstacles by running, jumping, and climbing), yoga for a strong mind, and other sports like basketball, and enjoys trekking. Akshay loves all kinds of sports.

He feels it's best to pick up your own body weight by engaging in rock climbing, hiking, skipping, or swinging. He doesn't pick up weights at all but does stretching exercises, yoga, and swimming as part of his fitness program. He believes in changing his exercises frequently, and trying out new things to kill monotony.

Akshay says that even after three decades of working out, he still doesn't have more than six abs. He does not resort to shortcuts to build his body and has no personal trainer—which is the way to go for celebrities of today.

3. No Vices for Mr Kumar

While James Bond is shown as a chain smoker on-screen, who also seizes every opportunity to have his martini, 'shaken and not stirred'. Our very own 'Mr Bond' doesn't get impressed at all by such habits, and rightly so. He wants to be 'real fit', and not 'reel fit'.

His motto is simple: 'Health matters most.' He avoids alcohol, smoking, nicotine, and caffeine in any form—coffee or tea. 'And if you smoke you will not have stamina, as well as you destroy your lungs forever,' he once said in an interview to *Bombay Times*.[16]

4. Home-Cooked Food Is the Best Food

He prefers home-cooked food and finds it to be the healthiest diet. For breakfast, it is parathas and a glass of milk for him. For mid-day snacks, it's usually some fruits and nuts. His lunch is a balanced meal of lentils, brown rice, wholesome veggies or lean meat and yogurt.

Akshay believes in having a balanced diet and eating the way our ancestors ate. 'Whatever your mother makes at home, is the best,' he will tell you. 'I eat anything my mother gives me, whether it is haldi doodh for immunity or warm water with honey for a bad throat.'[17]

The one thing that he has followed throughout his life and has really made a difference to him is eating dinner before sunset. His last meal of the day is a light combination of soup and sautéed vegetables. If he feels hungry after 7 p.m., he'd probably have an egg white omelette or soup

---

[16]https://timesofindia.indiatimes.com/entertainment/hindi/bollywood/news/Akshay-Kumar-After-32-years-of-working-out-I-still-dont-have-more-than-6-packs/articleshow/45258259.cms

[17]https://food.ndtv.com/health/akshay-kumar-turns-49-heres-his-diet-and-formula-for-the-fit-life-1436862

or something that is easy to digest. If he has to go out for dinner, he avoids carbs and focuses on proteins. No packaged or processed food for Mr Kumar as much as possible. He never diets, but takes all his meals on time.

5. **An Advise that Can Work**
Almost everyone, from dieticians and gym instructors to fitness gurus, push you against the wall by telling you to have protein shakes, supplements, boiled food without oil, and an absolute no to regular food. This may be possible to practice for a few days, but you cannot do this all your life. But, what Akshay Kumar does is highly workable. Eat well, eat in moderation, and eat on time. Avoid carbs to a large extent but don't kill yourself over it. Make it a part of your lifestyle which is sustainable, may be forever.

Daily Fitness Routine: The Natural Way

The best thing about Akshay's routine is that he follows no routine. In the sense, he cannot follow a pattern every day because of professional constraints. It is obvious that with crazy shooting, travel, and dubbing schedules, no actor can follow a set routine. Does that ring a bell? This is the lifestyle for most of us as well, the ones who work for a living, and Akshay's style is inspiring for all such people who are struggling to find their work-fitness balance. Yes, you too can do it. Just follow Akshay Kumar!

As someone dedicated to his fitness, he experiments with multiple kinds of exercise routines, preferring ones that require him to pick up his own body weight—like swinging and climbing trees as children do—than ones that require him to lift artificial weights. This exactly what functional fitness is all about. His equipment is simple: roman rings, pommel horse training for triceps, or a handstand for the ultimate shoulder strength. Again, I would like to reiterate that most of the training of even those in the armed forces is without too much of heavy-weight lifting or fashionable equipment. It is mostly with *'khaali haath'*.

Regarding food, Akshay says, 'Trust more in the parathas made by your mother than in protein shakes, pills, and supplements... Try not to take steroids.'[18] He not only bakes desserts, such as soufflé and layered white chocolate mousse, but also eats them; but in his own words, 'control mein.' Do it but in moderation, he advises… And that's what most of us don't do. In fitness and staying healthy…'slow and steady win the race.'

---

[18] http://blog.indiabriefs.com/akshay-kumar-redefining-fitness/

Managing Time

We have only 24 hours in a day—nothing less and nothing more. You need to have your priorities right for it. Akshay Kumar says that out of the twenty-four hours, eight should go to sleep, two to exercise, and the rest is available to do what you want—it is no rocket science, he feels.

If you love your work, you are never tired and energy automatically flows within. I also feel that when you get up early in the day like Akshay does by waking up at 5.30 a.m., you get a great head start and can pack in more productive hours during the day than those who wake up late. These are again pretty simple time management philosophies that can work.

Lean vs Bulky Muscles

Many people are left impressed by a bodybuilder's body, the kind that is marked with bulging muscles popping out of one's t-shirt. They think a lean body is not as good or powerful as a big body, but the truth is that muscle is just that—muscle. There is no such thing as bulky muscle or lean muscle. It holds the same amount of power inside. It is all just muscle under the big build, and since a lean-looking body is more attractive to many people today, why not stick to building lean instead of big?

Whether you are running on the beach, playing with your kids, or running to catch a train, it is easier to do it with a lean body than a big, bulky one. In other words, you are able to take on anything that comes your way without worrying about your body getting in the way or causing a problem. Your body needs to be functionally fit—that is the long and short of it.

'Indeed, many women are intimidated by the hyper-muscular, big, bad, buffed look.'

—TheRichest

A Strong Willpower

In the end, everything boils down to being able to focus and following it consistently with a strong willpower. In fact, many of us are not aware of our own capacity to take physical and mental challenges. Most people underestimate their capacity to go through a tough ordeal, whether physical or mental. But once someone is put in a tough situation, he/she fights it and comes out of it because of their will to survive.

There is a big difference in being cornered because of external factors and in putting yourself voluntarily in a tough situation. In the first situation, you have no choice because the external factors have put you in difficulty. Therefore you are in a do or die situation. Whereas when you volunteer, you have an option to move out. And that is what is difficult—to adopt a healthy lifestyle yourself and then staying on that track for a lifetime, despite having an option to quit. Akshay Kumar has volunteered to remain fit and has changed his lifestyle to achieve that forever.

'Exercise to stimulate, not to annihilate. The world wasn't formed in a day, and neither were we. Set small goals and build upon them.'

—*Lee Haney*

What can you learn from Akshay Kumar for your own fitness?

1. Make your fitness routine your lifestyle, and not a punishment.
2. Everyone, even the rich and the mighty, have only twenty-four hours in a day. You need to find just one hour in a day to exercise, and that is not difficult to achieve.
3. You don't have to opt for protein shakes and supplements to keep yourself fit. Akshay Kumar does not take any such products either.
4. Home-cooked food is the best for you. You can eat whatever you like as long as it is in moderation. Early to bed and early to rise—the tried and tested mantra is what works for Akshay and can work just as well for anyone who wants to remain healthy, wealthy, and wise.
5. He does not work out in gyms and does not lift weights at all. His exercise routine includes roman rings, parallel bars, and horizontal bars for chin-ups. Keep it simple and that is what works always.
6. You need to look fit and do not necessarily need to have a bulging body like that of a bodybuilder to prove it.

7. Akshay has his dinner before sunset and that is what he feels is the most important factor in not putting on weight and remaining fit.
8. A sound sleep of eight hours is very important. Nature repairs your body when you are asleep and that is very important for a fit body.
9. Wake up early and start your day with a head start over others.
10. Avoid alcohol and don't smoke. These are two things that can be very harmful to your body.
11. Make fitness routine a habit; all it takes is determination.

4

HEAD IN THE CLOUDS AND FEET FIRMLY ON THE GROUND

'When you taste super-success after tasting super-failure, there is huge relief.'

—Akshay Kumar

Everyone is ambitious and everyone wants to be successful. Especially in the show business which comes with immense glamour and star-following, who would like to be left out? It is the kind of profession that takes one to dizzying heights of success! It is very difficult to remain sober and grounded in an industry which puts you on such a high pedestal that people adore you, revere you, and wait to catch a glimpse of you. The flashing cameras and paparazzi i.e. the media chasing you all the time, constantly trying to keep a tab at every moment of your life, your story, your romances, and this desperate attention paid by them towards your personal life gives you a high which no other nectar, potion, or even alcohol can possibly give you.

You get fan mails, letters, bouquets, awards, and millions following you on Twitter. Many want to just touch and feel you. Some actors even receive letters from fans written in blood! You are presented as a larger-than-life persona to the masses. You have charisma; people welcome you with whistles and hooting when you come on a stage. You are a demigod for your fans, and there comes a point where you start thinking of yourself as God.

Akshay Kumar is also like any other mortal who is susceptible to the charms and intoxicatingly heady success of stardom. He is one of the most bankable actors, very handsome, fighting fit, and is adored by people. He is rich, and he makes producers rich and his films successful. He has more than 120 films under his belt. And you expect him not to throw tantrums? To not be snobbish, to not be arrogant, to not be looking down on people? But Akshay does none of that. It takes a very strong character and upbringing to remain sane in such a commanding position. You may not have a highly educated, sophisticated background, or may not have been brought up in the most expensive neighbourhood, yet you can be humble and respectful to others. You can be respectful even after a stupendous success—the success which you achieved after a lot of hard work, struggle, and at times humiliation, rejections and pulls and pressures of an industry which is very ruthless and an audience which is rarely forgiving.

For everyone who climbs the ladder successfully and manages to reach the top, the mantra is: You don't get successful by fooling around, but don't fool around when you become successful. Akshay Kumar has followed this dictum. He worked very hard to get where he is today and yet he has his feet firmly on ground.

'I'm not hungry for success. I am only hungry for good work, and that is how it is with most superstars. Every day I tell myself how fortunate I am to be where I am.'

—*Akshay Kumar*

No Jealousy, Only Envy

Akshay Kumar has always admired the work of other actors

and is certainly not in a race to beat them. Once he was asked if he was jealous at all of his contemporaries like Shah Rukh Khan, Salman Khan, and Aamir Khan, and if he kept a tab on their work. He responded by saying that he did keep a track of their films and even their philanthropic work but it is more out of respect for them. He believes in healthy jealousy i.e. envying their work, but not holding any grudge against his fellow superstars. So, when he looks up to them or sees their films, he has thoughts like: 'Wow, what a great shot, what a film. What a kind gesture.'[19]

He says that he does not follow their moves, so that he can beat them at it or anything as desperate as that. 'I never look at their successes and go, "Damn! That should have been me." I look at them and think, "Come on Akshay, if you want to stay in this industry, you better show your fans that you are worth it,"' he said.[20]

In fact, he has a very good chemistry with his contemporary, Salman Khan, who he feels is a very good human being. They always support each other and can bank on their friendship. 'Our equation is one of the most honest

---

[19] https://www.hindustantimes.com/bollywood/i-have-a-healthy-jealousy-for-the-khans-akshay-kumar/story-dTcfITC2q2T3nrtuzSQ4gK.html
[20] https://www.hindustantimes.com/bollywood/i-have-a-healthy-jealousy-for-the-khans-akshay-kumar/story-dTcfITC2q2T3nrtuzSQ4gK.html

ones in the industry. We let each other do our own thing, and admire each other's work from a distance,' he said once in an interview.

Being Open to Criticism

Akshay is very practical when it comes to understanding how fragile a film actor's career is. He has said, 'Stardom… has not gone to my head. When I achieve success, I see my children, my wife and my mother happy, and instinctively, I am filled with gratitude.'[21] He doesn't mind criticism, which is constructive in nature. He takes it like a feedback that can help him do better in the next film. Apart from feedback coming from the outside world, he has people he looks up to for feedback within his home—like his wife, Twinkle Khanna, a former actress who has seen the industry from close quarters since she is the daughter of Rajesh Khanna, Bollywood's first superstar, and her mother, Dimple Kapadia, too was a popular heroine of her times. And therefore, she can comment on Akshay's performance as an insider and also as one actor would do for another actor. But he also depends

---

[21] https://www.hindustantimes.com/bollywood/stardom-has-not-gone-to-my-head-akshay-kumar/story-FWoqxDdMA3mlDlhxyCHq5O.html

on his sister Alka, whom he is very close to, for an honest feedback. He feels that she is a good critic of his work because she watches his films as a non-filmy person and sometimes in a theatre 'with the rowdiest crowds watching a movie'. He feels that the opinions given by his sister tell him whether the movie will click with the audience or not.

It is very important for family members to give you their honest feedback instead of only praising you each time because that way you will never improve. At the same time, it's important that we are open to that feedback given by our loved ones, and take it positively. This will only help you take remedial actions and make your work and performance better with every passing day.

Actor Shahid Kapoor, son of eminent stage and film actor, Pankaj Kapur, too feels the same and likes to have an honest feedback on his work from his father. 'He [Pankaj Kapoor] doesn't say things till he actually means it. So, I wait for his compliments,' Shahid says,[22] adding that his father's constructive criticism gives him tips to become a better actor.

---

[22] http://www.dailyexcelsior.com/i-wait-for-my-fathers-compliments-on-my-work-shahid-kapoor/

> 'Life isn't about finding yourself. Life is about creating yourself.'
>
> —*George Bernard Shaw*

His Priorities Are Clear

Akshay is one of the fittest actors in the Indian film industry and that is because fitness is his priority. 'One should never jeopardize one's body for anyone or anything, not even for a film. If a movie required me to make drastic changes to my body, I would refuse it point blank.'[23] Many actors both male and female go through a strictly charted out diet plan for changing their physique and to lose or gain weight in a span of a few weeks—an idea that sounds absurd to ordinary people. Losing or gaining weight in a short time is very harmful for your health. But people label it simply as a professional hazard and leave it up to you to do it or not, but for Akshay it is a strict no. 'You've got only one body, if you don't nurture it now, don't expect it to support you

---

[23]https://www.hindustantimes.com/bollywood/i-have-a-healthy-jealousy-for-the-khans-akshay-kumar/story-dTcfITC2q2T3nrtuzSQ4gK.html

later,' he says.[24] Even building muscles in a short time and acquiring six-pack abs is also harmful because you cannot maintain that physique for a sustainable time period and you may have problems later.

Socializing in the showbiz is considered a vital part of the job. Most people including established stars see these parties as a part of networking and PR activity. Yes, these things do help when you meet people and socialize within the fraternity but Akshay Kumar does not attend late night parties as he gives priority to his family and health. He says, 'I always choose my health over having a good time.'[25] Well said, Mr Kumar.

He says that by now people know that even if he comes for their party, he will leave early as he has to catch up with his family and his sleep. You need to have confidence in yourself and your capabilities to go against the tide and come out as a winner. It also demonstrates your strong character and determination.

---

[24]https://www.hindustantimes.com/bollywood/i-have-a-healthy-jealousy-for-the-khans-akshay-kumar/story-dTcfITC2q2T3nrtuzSQ4gK.html
[25]https://www.hindustantimes.com/bollywood/i-have-a-healthy-jealousy-for-the-khans-akshay-kumar/story-dTcfITC2q2T3nrtuzSQ4gK.html

No Qualms Over His Humble Background

In one of the reality shows that Akshay had starred in, the organizers of the programme had invited some of his friends from his youth—a time when he was a nobody. These friends of his had regular jobs, while Akshay had become a superstar by then. Yet the way he greeted and hugged them, showed that he had no airs about himself. Most people when they become rich and famous forget their old friends, and sometimes even refuse to recognize them. To remember and acknowledge your old friends even after becoming successful is a great quality—especially today when people tend to be more selfish and self-centred.

Akshay never had an inferiority complex even when he was at the lower end of the achievement graph. He was happy and content with whatever he had. Now, this is the biggest thing one can have—contentment. You may be happy with very little or you can be very unhappy, disgruntled, and distressed with even a lot dropped in your lap by the almighty. The choice is yours.

Let me share an idea about happiness. I was watching a programme on one of the knowledge (infotainment) channels which was showing the fifty most expensive bathrooms in the world. The most expensive one as of today costs US$ 2.3

million, which is approximately a whopping ₹15 crore. The entire bathroom is made of gold—all of it! Now let us see who is happier and who is more content—a man living in a small flat with just one simple toilet, or a man with the most expensive bathroom?

Let us say the rich guy is suffering from severe constipation and has not had a bowel movement in several days despite sitting on 'the golden throne' for hours. He is uneasy, uncomfortable, and miserable, unable to eat anything for days. He may be happy because he is sitting in an air-conditioned golden toilet worth crores. But the man who has a simple toilet can clear his stomach every morning and have a hearty breakfast is content and happy. Just ponder over it. Something like having a plush bedroom and king-size bed means nothing if you can't even get proper sleep.

Akshay Kumar says that he was happy even when he stayed in a one-bedroom flat with his family in Chandni Chowk in Delhi and he is happy even now when God has given him so much. This is the greatest learning from the man who keeps his morale high even when tides are against him. This is a lesson for everyone: You don't reach the top of the ladder right at the beginning of your career. Say if you work in sales and marketing, you have to move on the streets in rain as well as heat. You are not paid as much as you expect, but your time comes eventually.

People who join the army don't become a general the first day. The first few years are formative years where you are made to rough out with the troops in the most difficult areas—snow, high altitudes, jungles, and deserts. You get your comforts as you move along.

'Happiness is a state of mind. It's just according to the way you look at things.'

—*Walt Disney*

He Never Forgets His Roots

Akshay Kumar is emotionally possessive about his old things, and has not forgotten his roots inspite of becoming a Bollywood superstar. He loves to preserve his 'firsts'—be it a picture, his old home, or his first car and his first bike. May be he wants to keep reminding himself where he rose from. I feel this is something that keeps you grounded and makes you feel grateful for all that you have.

Being nostalgic about his childhood days, he still

comes back to his one-bedroom flat in Chandni Chowk without anyone's knowledge. He says he wears a cap to go unrecognized in the lanes and move peacefully. He also loves eating langar from Gurudwara Sis Ganj Sahib, nearby, '...I come to Delhi quite often because I have a house here. I come quietly and stay a night there and leave in the morning,' he says. He seems to give a lot of emphasis to his roots, which is worth noting. 'That's where I came from, that's the place I belong to.'[26] Interestingly, he still has his old car, a Honda CRV, which he bought a long time back, and loves to drive it.

He is a man who earns in millions, but says his personal expense is not more than ₹5,000 per month. Mr Kumar owes it to frugal living and healthy thinking! For instance, his favourite perfume is Cool Water by Davidoff which is not a very expensive one to use. Sometimes he and his wife go to a restaurant in Mumbai for dinner and their bill is less than even ₹1,000.

---

[26]https://timesofindia.indiatimes.com/entertainment/hindi/bollywood/news/I-stay-in-Chandni-Chowk-at-times-Akshay/articleshow/8824183.cms

Head in the Clouds and Feet Firmly on the Ground

'We can never obtain peace in the outer world until we make peace with ourselves.'

—*Dalai Lama*

What can you learn from Akshay Kumar about humility?

1. Be envious, and not jealous of your competition. Be open to learn from others and admire good things in them rather than being jealous.
2. Be ambitious, but don't sacrifice your health and family life for it. Health is wealth and no amount of money can buy you health and happiness.
3. Don't ever neglect your family while pursuing a career or job. You may attain lots of wealth but you will never get back the time you missed spending with your child and family.
4. Listen to the suggestions given by your family as they are always well-meaning. Take it as constructive criticism and in a positive way.
5. Your career can go up and it can also go down—especially

in fragile professions like films. So, learn to keep your head in the clouds and keep your feet firmly on the ground.
6. Love and respect your parents and old friends. Don't forget they brought you up and stood by you when you were not famous.
7. Never forget your past and your humble beginnings, however successful you may become. These things will always make you feel good and grateful for what you have.
8. Happiness is a state of mind. Be grateful for what you have and don't cry over what you don't have. Thank God for the smallest of mercies.

5

TAKING RISKS, MAKING OPPORTUNITIES

'One of the greatest discoveries a man makes, one of his great surprises, is to find he can do what he was afraid he couldn't do.'

—Henry Ford

What does it mean by being brave? Is it only bravery in physical sense, that you require in say a battlefield, a boxing match, or a sword fight? Or is it also the courage of conviction? Another type of bravery can be the ability to take risk in business, profession, and calculated risks during any venture one undertakes. Therefore, bravery can have various meanings. A man or a woman who is physically brave and can take on immense pain and is prepared to get his or her jaw broken during a boxing match, may not be able to stand up for his rights and what he feels is correct. Alternatively, there can be someone who cannot pick a street fight with goons who take a jibe at him, or may be afraid to walk through a dark street, yet he may be able to take up the cause of the poor and start a campaign against a powerful mafia. It is difficult, if not impossible, to find a person who is 'all in all brave', meaning brave in every possible facet of life. So, a brave person can be summarized as one who takes risks and opens up various opportunities to excel in his life.

Akshay Kumar: A Man Who Takes Risks

Akshay Kumar is physically fit and morally sound and is also one to take risks within his professional domain. He is one of the few actors in the film industry who performs his own stunts. Other noteworthy actors who don't shy away from doing their own stunts are Ajay Devgn, Hrithik Roshan, Tiger Shroff, and John Abraham. There are some top actors in Hollywood too who do their own dangerous stunts. The line-up is impressive but list is again short; they are Tom Cruise, Jackie Chan, Matt Damon, Jason Statham, Arnold Schwarzenegger, and Sylvester Stallone.

One can narrate a number of mind-numbing stunts performed by Akshay that kept the audience on the edge of their seats. One such was in the film *Ashaant* (1993) where he had to fight the villain, played by Puneet Issar, while hanging from a flying helicopter. Recollecting the stunt, Puneet Issar said in an interview to *The Indian Express*: 'I was fighting on ground with Akshay when the helicopter comes in and I try to escape. The chopper was about six to seven feet high in the air and I had to jump on to the rope, climb it and then enter the chopper. Akshay was to follow suit and…the chopper would take off with me inside and Akshay hanging from the rope. We both did the stunts ourselves.'[27] Issar had also said that though Akshay did wear a safety harness belt, still it was a very risky affair.

One cannot take performing stunts lightly, even if they appear simple or are small in nature. Akshay Kumar understands this very well and is equally careful with every stunt. This could be an offshoot of his training in martial arts where the instructor always keeps a check on your emotions and mental stability whenever you get into a fighting match.

---

[27]https://indianexpress.com/article/entertainment/bollywood/how-akshay-kumar-pulled-off-a-dangerous-helicopter-stunt-in-ashaant-watch-video-4363436/

Every such scene is like a real-time stunt where any of the two participants can get injured.

While shooting for his film *Holiday: A Soldier Is Never Off Duty*, Akshay recalls in an interview given to *India Today* that the movie was heavily action-oriented and the fact that they never entered any studio or set but did all the action sequences in actual locations, including even on a ship. He says that it was fun working with a director like A.R. Murugadoss who is a real action director. For the film, they also engaged Greg Powell, the action director who has directed stunts for the James Bond and Harry Potter films.

Probably because of his habit of being careful, Akshay has never been injured seriously. He did develop a nagging back problem when he did a 'military press' lift in the 1996 film, *Khiladiyon Ka Khiladi*, with the WWE star 'the Undertaker' who weighed 320 pounds or approximately 150 kg. It caused his back to give out. It was so severe an injury that he still suffers from its pain sometimes even now.

Stars like Hrithik Roshan and Shah Rukh Khan too have had their fair share of injuries during film shootings. The most serious one for Hrithik was when he injured his head in Phuket while shooting for *Bang Bang*, requiring him to undergo brain surgery. On the sets of *Krrish*, Hrithik survived a fatal fall while jumping off a skyscraper when the supporting wire snapped. Luckily for him, his fall was broken when he landed on a canopy which had been kept open by one of the shops due to the light drizzle that was expected on the day the mishap happened.

Shah Rukh Khan has been injured during fight sequences several times and says that he prays to God to give him another set of bones because he has several of them in bad shape. He has had broken ribs, knee, and neck injuries. He has had several surgeries done on him because of accidents on the sets.

A Daredevil to the Core

Some of the stunts that Akshay has performed in his career have been very dangerous. For instance in *Khiladi 420*, he climbs on top of an aircraft and jumps on to a hot air balloon below which is being used by the villain to highjack and kidnap the heroine. During the shooting of *Singh Is Kinng*, Akshay jumped from one elevator to another in a shopping mall at a height of 110 feet. Here's the shocking part—there was no harness or net used.

To save his heroine, Raveena Tandon, while shooting for *Keemat*, Akshay set fire to his legs in response to a pack of goons carrying sharp objects, for a scene. He's shown such daredevilry on a few live occasions too, once in the title song of the film, *Barood* and once at the unveiling of the Levi's 501 Jeans line.[28]

Taking Professional Risks

When you are doing well and are cruising at a steady pace, you want the status quo to be maintained. Many people do not want any disruptions in their work space. And a career as risky as one in the showbiz prompts people to be ever more cautious; every move you make, every film you chose, whom you work with, which production house, who your co-stars are, and what kind of story it is—is like playing chess, calculating each move and watching your own step. While most may take this conventional approach, there are a few who have a mighty heart and are prepared to experiment with new storylines—some bold, some exciting, and some which may not even fit in your type of an image.

Rishi Kapoor had said that when he was approached to play the role of 'Rauf Lala', which is a negative character, he refused it point blank. The film was being made by Karan

---

[28] http://thekhiladizone.blogspot.in/2009/03/akshay-kumars-top-10-stunts.html

Johar and he wanted Rishi to play that role of a pimp. Later in a literature festival, Rishi had said 'I asked Karan Johar, do I look like a pimp to you? I am not going to do this silly role where I am supplying young girls.' But Karan was adamant and asked him to do a look test. Rishi Kapoor took the risk and agreed for the look test, and rest as they say is history. He pulled it off so well that it was one of the selling points of the movie. He had also played a schoolteacher in *Do Dooni Char* which again was something very different from the image he had grown accustomed to in all the decades he had worked.

Most actors take the risk of changing their image and looks usually only when they have done it all and passed their prime. But Akshay Kumar's story is different. He is still a mainstream actor who plays the hero. He still has the young hero's image who can play lead roles, including action ones. Not many would like to meddle with that—and take the risk of doing off-beat characters as opposed to the conventional hero.

For him, the going was good and he could have stuck to his groove and kept on doing roles that matched his image. Yet he is experimenting with different types of storylines and some are even risky in the commercial cinema space. He had started out as a hero and had proved his prowess as an action lead hero during the first few years of his career. He has done more than 120 films out of which there are twenty-plus movies which are of action nature. The most memorable such roles are in films like *Khiladi* (1992), *Mr. Bond* (1992), *Ashaant* (1993), *Elaan* (1994), *Mohra* (1994), *Suhaag* (1994), *Angarey* (1998), *Barood* (1998), and then four more films in the Khiladi series up to the year 2000.

By 2000, he had established himself very well and started accepting action comedy films like *Awara Paagal Deewana* (2002), while doing romantic films like *Dhadkan* (2000), *Ek Rishta* (2001), *Andaaz* (2003), etc.

He has, thereafter, not stuck to any stereotype and has gone all guns blazing with comedy and action. Some comedy films worth mentioning here are: *Hera Pheri* (2000), *Bhagam Bhag* (2006), *Bhool Bhulaiyaa* (2007), *Mujhse Shaadi Karogi* (2004), *Garam Masala* (2005), *Singh Is Kinng* (2008), *Welcome* (2007) *Phir Hera Pheri* (2006), *Khatta Meetha* (2010), *Singh Is Bliing* (2015), and the Housefull series.

In between he has also done some serious roles to demonstrate his acting prowess and ended up giving fine performances in films like *Namastey London* (2007), *OMG: Oh My God* (2012), *Special 26* (2013), etc. The year 2015 saw him in movies like *Gabbar Is Back*, *Baby*, and *Brothers*, each one was of a different genre and Akshay gave performances that were appreciated by many.

The year 2016 saw two of his best movies that put forth his brilliant acting skills—*Rustom* and *Airlift*, both inspired by real life incidents.

Akshay admits that comedy is the most difficult of the genres to pull off; it takes great timing and a sense of extempore reactions. Also, he dabbled in action comedy like Jackie Chan is known to, which is even more difficult; case in point: *Rowdy Rathore*.

Exploring New Avenues

Once a daredevil always a daredevil—this stands true for Mr Kumar. It was because of this that he was made the first host of *Fear Factor: Khatron Ke Khiladi*, the Indian franchise of the stunt reality game show, based on the American program *Fear Factor*. The series was first launched in India in 2006, and it received a great response from the viewers. The second season of the show was launched about two years later. Akshay successfully hosted first, second, and fourth season of the show.

Rohit Shetty, one of the successful action directors in Bollywood hosted this show too. He found it very challenging and difficult because shooting with seasoned actors who have the knowledge of stunt performance is much easier than dealing with first-time performers for this reality show. In an interview, Shetty revealed that it was mentally taxing to be a part of the stunt-based reality show. 'When you are performing with stuntmen or Ajay [Devgn], who has been doing stunts for many years, you are not that stressed out. But on the show you have twelve people who have never done stunts. You are making them perform stunts. There is stress, because you need to take care and make sure nothing goes wrong,' he says.[29]

Shetty's perspective helps us understand the difficulties that Akshay too must have faced while hosting the show for three seasons and making mainstream films simultaneously.

Putting Your Money Where Your Mouth Is

I have seen former CEOs of multinational corporations dealing with their company products rather boldly and spending lavishly as they were working for the company and the risk taken was not personal. But the same people when they started their own venture as a start-up behaved very differently. Since, by then, it was their own money that was

---

[29]https://www.ndtv.com/entertainment/khatron-ke-khiladi-why-rohit-shetty-thinks-the-stunts-based-show-is-difficult-1728003

involved they were very cautious, frugal, and sometimes very fearful about taking bold decisions.

Similarly, it is one thing to act according to a production house-funded and conceived story for a film and it is quite different to produce your own film. Film projects are the riskiest kind of products because you have no set formula for a hit film.

Akshay Kumar started his own production house in 2008. It was named after his father Hari Om Bhatia. In an interview at the time he said that under Hari Om Productions he will be producing different kinds of films. Akshay confirmed that he was turning producer and said, 'I think it's finally time that I took the leap. The past eighteen years in the industry have been a great learning experience and I think I have enough knowledge to attempt my own production house.'[30] Akshay wanted to be a producer because he wanted to provide world-class cinema in India. The partners in the production house are Akshay Kumar, his mother, Aruna Bhatia, and his wife, Twinkle Khanna. They have produced more than a dozen films till date. Some of the hits were: *Singh Is Kinng, Patiala House, OMG: Oh My God, Khiladi 786, Holiday: A Solider Is*

---

[30] http://www.bollywoodmantra.com/news/akshay-kumar-turns-producer-with-hari-om-productions/2329/

Never Off Duty, *Airlift*, *Rustom*, and *Pad Man*.

This takes a different kind of courage which also means business courage, courage of your own convictions, and the courage to take financial risks, of course all are calculated risks. As a producer you have the freedom to experiment with different subjects, listen to your heart and produce films that you find relevant to the times. There are profits to share but you sure have the risk of losing your money, and sometimes sleep too. Akshay has demonstrated that he not only has physical courage but has gradually acquired with his film experience and maturity, business courage too.

'It is curious that physical courage should be so common in the world and moral courage so rare.'

—Mark Twain

Gayatri Mantra Is His Spiritual Strength

He is a religious person and chants the Gayatri Mantra before doing any stunt. It gives him inner strength. While shooting for *Khatron Ke Khiladi* in 2008, he taught chanting of the mantra to all the thirteen participants, explaining to them that it provides inner strength. He says, 'Whenever I do my stunts, I chant the Gayatri Mantra in my mind. I strongly believe that our body is animated by life energy. According to India's science of sound healing, you can gather and direct that healing life force through the power of sacred sound.'[31]

What can you learn from Akshay Kumar about being brave?

1. Bravado is of two kinds: Physical bravery, as in a battlefield or a boxing match; and the other one is mental tenacity which gives you moral courage and also the ability to take risks in your profession. Akshay Kumar displays both.
2. Being a martial art enthusiast and a sportsman, he has demonstrated great prowess as an action hero. He performs his stunts himself, very much like Jackie Chan.
3. He has also experimented with different types of roles, from the classic Khiladi action films to serious roles like in *Rustom* and *Airlift*, he has also done comedy successfully

---

[31] https://www.thehindu.com/todays-paper/tp-national/tp-newdelhi/ Beating-fear-with-faith-and-prayer/article15261448.ece

in many films, such as *Bhool Bhulayiaa* and *Hera Pheri*. One must try different things professionally and should step out of his/her comfort zone.
4. One can learn a great lesson from Akshay's career of not making education an impediment, especially in the era of entrepreneurs. An engineer can start a fitness studio and a doctor can get into food business. A lot of different permutations are possible.
5. One must also try different avenues and new genres. Despite having a successful Bollywood career, Akshay has shown great risk-taking ability by taking on reality shows like *Khatron Ke Khiladi*.
6. Another aspect of life is to invest your own money into your profession. This requires not only confidence in yourself and mastering your craft but also a bit of risk-taking capacity. Today, the world is opening to opportunities and people who achieve success in one business can try to diversify into different areas and avenues.
7. 'No pain, no gain' is what he has been able to demonstrate with his long career of twenty-five years. He has had his share of flops and hits, and yet carries on regardless. As such, the show business is an unpredictable place with

lots of hits and misses. To survive in such an industry one requires courage and conviction.
8. Self-discipline is the key to success in every profession. In a world which is getting more and more difficult professionally due to fierce competition, you have to be disciplined to not only do well but also to survive.

6

THE ULTIMATE SUCCESS FORMULA
Practice Professionalism

'Opportunities don't happen. You create them.'

—Chris Grosser

To do well in life, one must have certain skills and based on that one acquires a craft. For instance, a carpenter first learns carpentry and as he gains more and more experience he acquires the craft and becomes a craftsman. Once a carpenter starts making furniture and excels at it, he needs to start selling it and gradually make the whole business profitable. He has to ensure that he produces certain number of pieces in a week to make the business viable. Time for production and optimization are two important ingredients to make your business viable—in this case it is craft and business converge.

This is the key to success and generating money. You may acquire a technology from abroad, but to make a product at a price which can sell in the market and generate profits is independent of the level of technology. It depends on how efficiently you can deploy that technology and produce a quality product.

Akshay Kumar's Business Model

Being in the film business for the last twenty-five years, Akshay Kumar has learnt the craft well enough and has also gained to understand how to best use money in this profession. Several actors and stars have ventured into film production and have used their star power and marketing techniques to make their films deliver on the box office and give them returns on their investment.

Akshay Kumar's business model is a little different. He banks on reducing the production cost, and not so much on other things like release date, market hype, etc. He is of the firm belief that if a movie can be finished in a certain time frame, the production cost can be minimized. In addition, if he is the producer himself, he sometimes doesn't charge any money for his work, to bring down the production cost drastically. What he takes is a share in the profits, which depends on the film's run at the box office. *Airlift* was made on this model, and the film did good business.

He understands that the cost of the lead male actor and other major actors is the biggest expense in the budget. An A-list actor can charge anything from ₹10 crore to ₹40 crore for a film. There is no fixed fee as such but the figure is high because neither the actor knows how much to ask, nor the producer knows how much to pay. This is because there is no certainty regarding the outcome of a film in terms of success and the kind of money it would generate. Akshay Kumar understands that artiste's cost is the biggest burden on the budget, so he feels that if he removes this burden from his films then there can never be a flop.

'I have a simple logic. I am the producer of the film, so I get money from my company to make the film, so my fee is zero. I make the film in say ₹15–20 crore. We sell the film and the film's cost gets covered in satellite rights. Then whatever business the film does is my fee. Sometimes the film does well, other times not. But there is no loss whatsoever,' he says.[32]

---

[32]https://www.pressreader.com/india/deccan-chronicle/20141109/283124247175376

Akshay also stresses on better planning before the shoot begins to reduce the cost further. 'The cost of production only goes high when you don't know your script, when you take 260 days for a film shoot. Many people take almost 300 days to shoot a film and people think *"Yeh hai kamal ki film."* I shoot my films in 40–50 days.'[33]

He himself banks on good planning and working strictly according to a pre-planned schedule. He finished Neeraj Pandey's film, *Baby*, in thirty-two days. He says that if the director has his script ready in every respect, thereafter, it is not difficult to shoot in a shorter time, 'For *Mission Impossible*, Tom Cruise had shot for just 47 days because the script was flawless and everyone knew what was to be done. Is there any Bollywood film that is larger than *MI*? Then why are we taking 280 days to complete one?'[34]

Moreover, he gives their due to everyone who is a part of his films. Writers are often not given their due importance in terms of money, but he bats for their share in the success of the film. 'I am making three to four films and I pay my writers well. Again, they can also go for profit sharing. If the

---

[33] https://www.pressreader.com/india/deccan-chronicle/ 20141109/ 283124247175376

[34] http://www.dnaindia.com/entertainment/interview-i-m-still-greedy-akshay-kumar-2032044

film works well, they can ask for their cut in the profit.'[35] That's for sure a win-win model for all stakeholders. His sure-shot success mantra, therefore, is to either make your own film or go for profit-sharing.

'A generation ago, the image was that you had to trample everyone else down to succeed; but I don't believe that makes good business sense.'

—Richard Branson

Professionalism Is Important

One definitely needs to know who is important in your business. Many actors who were big stars were eased out because they were not only a pain to the producer, but they were also a drain on their finances. A producer is the one who takes the risk and if he is going to make a loss the whole business will go for a toss.

Akshay Kumar is very sharp to understand this and says,

---

[35]https://tribune.com.pk/story/365580/akshay-kumar-talks-business/

'In this industry, it's not about how good an actor you are. It's all about how good you are to your producer,' he says, adding, 'in my nearly twenty-six years in this business, I have learnt this. It's how well you protect your producer that matters.'[36]

His producers are more than happy because Akshay is punctual, courteous, does his job well, and ensures that their interest is first in his mind. What more can you ask for? He throws no tantrums, does not show off, or have snobbish behaviour.

Akshay is frank enough to know his strengths and weaknesses. There was a time when he had more than a dozen back-to-back flops and yet he had some good films in hand. Owing to such ups and downs, he has today grown into a very fine actor in his quarter of a century long career. That's primarily because he always understood the pain point of producers and focused on supporting them to the hilt.

He always kept his optimism intact and did not get affected too much by the hits and misses of his career. He has said, 'My whole career has been about ups and downs. On the downs too, it's been great.'[37]

---

[36] http://www.forbesindia.com/printcontent/45259
[37] http://www.forbesindia.com/printcontent/45259

Producers remain his priority. 'This is the only industry where the boss is a naukar (servant),' says Kumar, adding, 'the producer is standing outside your van which he gave you! How the hell did he land outside?' Akshay thus instructed his business manager to never make a producer stand outside. That's apparently the reason why none of his films remain incomplete or canned, in his 120-plus-films career. Kumar further believes that whatever be the case, the studio which buys the final film should never be made to suffer losses.

Keen Business Sense

I always say that management is nothing but common sense. In business schools we teach business through case studies. What do you actually learn from a case study? You learn who did, what, how and when and learn from other's experience. You should also learn from other's mistakes. Why must you make mistakes and then learn from those, which will be a very costly model of learning.

Outsourcing is something that works very well in every field. Franchisee model is a type of outsourcing too. The business process outsourcing is an industry by itself. As a company, you concentrate on your core competence and let someone else do data processing or voice calls on your behalf. For instance, today large telecom companies ask another company to build towers, yet another one to handle and maintain the hardware and switches, someone else looks after billing, and yet another company looks after the sale and retail. The name is that of the telecom company but there are a number of different components that play together. The head company looks after the marketing, branding, and integration too in some cases and looks at the quality control, customer service, and overall revenue model.

Akshay learnt the art of outsourcing from my friend, Vikas Oberoi, who runs a realty business. He says he has improvised the outsourcing model in film-making and it is working well for Akshay.

'Improvisation in the jazz sense—like the business sense—is not formless. It is built on a skill set. Jazz, for example, involves selecting a tune.'

—John Kao

Teeth to Tail Ratio

This is an important military principle. The teeth are the fighting component and tail is the logistics and maintenance. Though there is always a tug of war going on between how much of teeth and how much of tail, the general idea is to cut and minimize the overall number. Tail often needs to be trimmed and many business houses do this too. For instance, if marketing is the job of the company, you need more emphasis on the guys selling the product than who are doing the human resource function or administrative staff.

Akshay keeps his staff very lean and mean. Despite his status in the industry, Kumar says he has just four or five key people as staff. And his outsourcing model allows him to keep his set-up lean and mean. Even when it comes to partnerships, he likes to be upfront and if it is not working out, he prefers to amicably end the partnership. And that's why Oberoi, a successful businessman himself, applauds Kumar's business sense: 'Akshay could match an MBA in business, dollar to dollar, and probably beat them because he's got more than that. Everything put together, he's better than many of the trained businessmen I have come across.'[38]

---

[38] http://www.forbesindia.com/printcontent/45259

Telescoping Time and Work

Akshay Kumar goes into details in detail! I am not sure how many actors would be doing this. He plans his shooting in the most optimized way. He gives block dates to one producer for say twenty days at a stretch, so that he can shoot it continuously and cover a large part of it in one go. The next set of dates he gives to another producer, say for twenty-five days. This, he believes, helps the first film-maker to edit the shooting done in the first block and be ready for the next phase of shooting, while he is shooting for the second film. This kind of meticulous planning and execution allows him to finish three to four films in a year, which is more than most of his peers.

This process is somewhat similar to the concept of assembly line production created by Henry Ford which revolutionized the manufacturing process almost a century ago. In this concept, instead of workers going to the work, work was brought to them on a conveyer belt. Ford could roll out thousands of cars from his factories in a short time. His first moving assembly line was a boon as it simplified assembly of the Ford Model T's 3,000 parts by breaking it into eighty-four distinct steps performed by groups of workers as a rope pulled the vehicle chassis down the line. It dropped the assembly time for a single vehicle from twelve hours to about ninety minutes! By reducing the money, time, and manpower needed to build cars, Ford was able to drop the price of the Model T from $850 to less than $300. For the first time in history, quality vehicles were affordable to the masses. Eventually, Ford built a Model T *every 24 seconds and sold more than 15 million worldwide by 1927*, accounting for half of all automobiles sold then.

Akshay Kumar probably did that in his film-making business, and has impressed his distributors with his philosophy of a professional who understands his craft and delivers as an actor and on time.

'Optimize your time, don't just manage it!'

—*Rosalene Glickman*

What can you learn from Akshay Kumar about doing the right things in your profession?

1. You must learn your craft well and excel in it too. But you must also know how to best deploy your craftsmanship to get the best product at the optimum cost. Time for production and optimization are two important ingredients to make your business viable.
2. Your product will never fail or make losses if your cost is optimized and you make it at a cheaper cost than your competition.
3. You should know who the most important person in the business chain is and focus on that. From who brings value to the business to who brings money to the business are all important factors. Critically identify that individual in the value chain and keep him on your right side always.
4. Your immediate professional circle must also know who is important for your progress and they must treat that entity with equal courtesy and be responsive towards him.
5. Learn from other's mistakes. Don't reinvent the wheel. Observe where others have gone wrong and don't make the same mistake in your professional work.
6. Concentrate on your core competence and let the 'other

work' be outsourced. Outsourcing allows people who are best at their task to do it for you and you need to integrate everything and focus on business rather than getting involved in everything or doing it by yourself. It is cheaper, more efficient, and allows you breathing time as well as strategic thinking.
7. Keep your organization lean and mean. Don't have too many people with you and around you. You save on salaries and avoid duplication as well as clutter. Too many cooks spoil the broth.
8. Optimize your time and production. Come up with creative ideas applicable to your business to reduce the time for manufacturing or doing the job. This brings in efficiency and, eventually, better returns on investment.

7

THE WINNING TRAITS
Versatile, Disruptive, and Bankable

'It is a law of nature we overlook, that intellectual versatility is the compensation for change, danger, and trouble.'

—H.G. Wells

Being versatile and disruptive are the two most important ingredients in the art and craft domain. It is important to excel but it is more important to excel differently. Versatility explains your being multitalented or being flexible and adaptable. Disruptive takes you a notch higher where you break rules, you are unconventional, experimentative, avant-garde, and unorthodox. You simply do things which may not have been done till now. These may be radically different, risky, groundbreaking, and even revolutionary.

Hindi cinema has come of age, but not many artistes take advantage of this fact. The most important thing in show business today is that the Indian 'mass audience' has changed too. It has matured. They want to see something different, something which has not been experienced before. They are looking for contrasts, and at times for films to go overboard too. Cinematography, stunts, special effects, and every technical support required on celluloid is nowadays available to a director and a storyteller in Indian cinema as much as it is available to Steven Spielberg or Christopher Nolan in Hollywood. It is the mindset of the producers, directors, and actors that has to evolve and be accepting of disruptive ideas.

Hindi cinema is coming up with brilliant plots, excellent stories, and themes like never before. People want fresh faces in lead roles and, therefore, well-established actors need to reinvent themselves and move out of their shallow grooves. All good actors always say 'my best is yet to come'. The reason is that they are looking for something different, something exciting and something that will appeal to the audience like never before.

Anupam Kher is also one actor who has done very unconventional roles. From taking up the role of a much older man, when he himself was only twenty-eight, in *Saaransh* to playing an alcoholic father in *Daddy*, a comedian in several films and a police commissioner in *A Wednesday*, he has never stopped reinventing himself. Some critics call him the chameleon who can change his reflections instantly. Akshay Kumar, a bankable star, too has delivered some very fine and versatile performances—from action to comedy to intense characters, he has done it all.

Mr Versatile, Mr Disruptor

So far Akshay Kumar has starred in over 120 films. And he has played a variety of roles in them. From starting out as an action hero, he later went on to do a string of comedies like *Hera Pheri* and *Bhool Bhulaiyaa*, and moved further on to intense dramas such as *Rustom* and *Airlift*. Kumar has done it all.

A look at some of the characters he has played in his recent films, gives a clear sense that he has definitely tried to play different roles and entertain people. In *Special 26*, he played a con man, a part of a group who pose as CBI officers and loot people; in *Airlift*, he was a real-life character who had rescued fellow Indians stranded in Kuwait after the Iraqi invasion in 1990. In *Gabbar Is Back*, he played a character who fights corruption in the system without being a uniformed man. In *Rustom*, also based on a true incident that rocked the nation in 1959, he played an Indian Navy officer. In between he also starred in commercial entertainers like the Housefull series, *Singh Is Kinng*, *Entertainment*, etc. His upcoming films promise to be as varied with *Kesari*, *2.0*, *Gold*, and *Housefull 4* in the pipeline.

Akshay says, 'I think it's my action hero image that makes me funnier. Like how when angry young man Amitabh Bachchan would do comedies, people would enjoy that... I make it a point to do a variety of roles because I don't want to just play a typical hero.'[39]

For Akshay, playing a common man and picking up stories from real life for the big screen has surely become his success mantra. Experimenting with your own money (as co-producer of films) and taking on groundbreaking and disruptive subjects like *Toilet: Ek Prem Katha* and *Pad Man* requires self-confidence and a deep understanding of the trade.

Akshay also stated that over the years, marketing has become an integral part of a film. It is in fact a big thing.

---

[39] https://www.deccanchronicle.com/141109/entertainment-bollywood/article/%E2%80%98my-life-boring%E2%80%99

'Marketing works for the first three days and content works after those three days. So it is very important to have the right content as well,' he said in an interview.[40]

I feel what needs to be appreciated the most about him is that he has got his finger on the pulse of such a complex business, and it is no joke. He is probably the shrewdest actor-producer combination out there.

Actor Suniel Shetty who has worked with him in hit films like *Mohra*, *Dhadkan*, *Hera Pheri*, among others, vouches for Akshay's versatility. 'Akshay is a very versatile actor. Whether it is in *Baby*, *Airlift*, or *Holiday*, he has carved that niche for himself because he looks like an officer and a gentleman,' said Suniel.[41]

'I refuse to be typecast, and I'll have a go at anything so long as it's different, challenging, hard work and demands great versatility.'

—Pete Postlethwaite

---

[40] https://www.news18.com/news/india/biggest-burden-on-a-film-is-its-artists-akshay-465564.html

[41] http://movies.ndtv.com/bollywood/akshay-kumar-is-a-versatile-actor-says-suniel-shetty-1271661

Bankable Star

Special 26, *Airlift*, and *Jolly LL.B 2* are some obvious examples of offbeat topics becoming successful films. Indian cinema as a whole is undergoing a change. While many of the big budget films with superstars are flopping—for instance, Salman Khan's *Tubelight* and Shah Rukh Khan's *Jab Harry Met Sejal*; small scale movies are emerging as sleeper hits, such as *A Death In The Gunj*, *Toilet: Ek Prem Katha*, *Secret Superstar*, etc. The time is ripe for film-makers to experiment and actors can give in their best shot at performances too. And Akshay is making the most of this latest trend. He shed his macho image, wore slippers and pyjamas, and got into the skin of a man we can find at any nook or corner of our streets. This is a character that has simple dreams and common problems. He spoke our language and returned with a broken bone if attacked by goons on the road. That's how Akshay revamped his image, which was once about being a one-man-army on-screen.

However, there is a background story to the drastic change that Akshay Kumar's film repertoire went through. This was revealed in one of the episodes of *Koffee with Karan* where Akshay appeared with his wife, Twinkle Khanna, by his side. While there were many insights shared by the couple about their chemistry, one thing that left the audience surprised was how Twinkle motivated Akshay to change the kind of films he was doing and to bring quality in them. Twinkle revealed that she had put a condition for Akshay, 'I told him I won't have a second child if he doesn't start doing sensible movies.'[42] This despite the fact that Akshay had established himself as a master of action and comedy by then. But it seems Twinkle wanted him to grow, just like his audience. A closer look at Akshay's films for the past 5–6 years will only make you realize that he, indeed, has grown as an actor, and he has played smart in terms of script selection and has rarely missed the bullseye, of late.

If you talk to producers and distributors in Bollywood about Akshay Kumar and they will vouch for his bankable star status. On an average, he does 3–4 films a year which have low production cost and are usually focused on a larger social cause. Thanks to his planning and astute business sense on content and marketing, most of them go on to become a hit at the box office. Most of his recent films have entered the 100-crore club: *Toilet: Ek Prem Katha* (₹168 cr), *Jolly LL.B 2* (₹149 cr), *Rustom* (₹173 cr), *Rowdy Rathore* (₹180 cr), *Rustom* (₹173 cr), *Airlift* (₹166 cr), *Holiday* (₹151 cr), *Housefull 2*

---

[42] https://www.telegraphindia.com/1161113/jsp/t2/story_118859.jsp

(₹153 cr), and *Housefull 3* (₹150 cr).[43]

Kumar rules the box office even after a quarter of a century, and is known as one of the most bankable stars in the business, along with the three Khans—Salman, Shah Rukh, and Aamir.

Spotting a Trend

To say that Akshay spots the upcoming trend and becomes a trendsetter won't be wrong. He turned to comedy when it was still only the forte of comedians and not something that the lead actors did. His association with Priyadarshan and the hits that came from it, such as *Hera Pheri*, *Bhagam Bhag*, *Bhool Bhulaiyaa*, and more, are proof of his successful comic timing. Soon his contemporaries followed suit and turned to comedy too. But by then Akshay had shed it all, even action, and had started playing a common man in his films.

Discipline as an Attitude

I feel this is a very important thing to learn from Akshay Kumar. He does four films in a year whereas many top stars in his league do one and some do one in even two years.

---

[43] Gross collection. Source: https://boxofficeindia.com/actor.php?actorid=2

Mind you, he still manages a week-long vacation once in three months and a long six-week holiday once a year. Many people in a 9 to 5 job find time management a great challenge; where as an actor's life is pretty stressful and hectic with travels, shooting at odd times, yet Akshay manages it well. Everyone has twenty-four hours in a day, it is how you organize yourself is what matters the most. Film industry works on a budget and the actor who can give best returns on the money invested by his producer is the king. No producer wants to prolong a project because each day costs money. This is one fundamental principle that is taught in project management where you have to monitor the execution of a project on a day-to-day basis and ensure that deadlines are met. Look at our own country, where most projects get delayed and there are costs exceeding budgets in most projects. Such an actor who is disciplined to the core is a producer's delight and as a team they optimize shooting schedule and it's a win-win for both the actor and the producer.

A hard core disciplinarian in his professional life, Akshay applies the same rule to his personal life as well. 'My life is quite boring. I don't have tea or coffee. I neither smoke nor indulge in hard drinks or drugs... But I love eating, especially sweets. All rumours about me avoiding sweets are completely fake. Just that I eat in the afternoon and avoid them at night.

Because you have the whole day to digest the food, while at night you simply store sugar in your body,' he says.[44]

'Living with fear stops us taking risks, and if you don't go out on the branch, you're never going to get the best fruit.'

—Sarah Parish

What you can learn from Akshay Kumar about versatility and being bankable?

1. To do well in any field in today's competitive environment one has to keep reinventing oneself.
2. You have to keep observing around you and see what others are doing and try to do things differently.
3. Learn to experiment in your profession and take a bit of risk. Akshay Kumar started as an action hero, shifted to comedy, and then to suave roles like in *Rustom*, and then a boy-next-door character in *Toilet: Ek Prem Katha*. In the

---

[44] https://www.deccanchronicle.com/141109/entertainment-bollywood/article/%E2%80%98my-life-boring%E2%80%99

upcoming *2.0* he is starring in a negative role opposite Rajinikanth.
4. Understand and appreciate the trends in your line of work. Like Akshay realized that small budget films with a good story line can be a profitable as well as satisfying work for an actor as well as the producer of the film.
5. Be disruptive, think disruptive because today everyone is thinking and your success depends on how out of the box you are prepared to go.
6. Earn money and also learn to spend it in style if you have earned it. Akshay has expensive cars which he can afford now. At the beginning of his career he may not have had that luxury. So, make hay when the sun shines.
7. Don't be greedy and think of yourself only. Think of the collaborators and others who contribute to the project. Especially of the person who has put in his money for you. It has to be a win-win situation. Think of collective gain and profits so that everyone is happy and satisfied.

8

BEYOND PROFESSIONAL SUCCESS
The Personal Side of Akshay Kumar

'It's all about quality of life and finding a happy balance between work and friends and family.'

—Philip Green

My Father, My Hero

Akshay Kumar's father, Hari Om Bhatia, was a soldier in the Indian Army and was majorly into wrestling even before joining the army. He left the army to join UNICEF in Delhi, where Akshay was born. After three years in Delhi he was transferred to Mumbai. They lived in a small rented accommodation which had kitchen on one side and a dining table and the bathroom on the other side and a room in the middle. It was not a very big way to begin life; moreover, Akshay had little interest in studies. He was fond of games and his father realized that he would be best suited for a sports-related profession. Even today, Akshay believes that his father was his biggest emotional support.

He lost his father in the year 2000 to cancer. He was a star by then and he did all that he could for his treatment but couldn't save him. 'I was most attached to him. He gave me company in everything I did. When I would represent volleyball in school, he would be the only father who would be there. He would come and watch and bring water and energy drinks for me and even my opponents. I am here today only because of his decision to allow me to go to Bangkok and learn martial arts against forcing me to study,' he says.[45]

Talking of his younger days and his family before marriage he says, 'There is no film we missed seeing as a family. Every Saturday, my dad, mom, sister and I would go and watch a movie... My dad was a big fan of Dharmendra and Dara

---

[45] https://timesofindia.indiatimes.com/entertainment/hindi/bollywood/news/Ive-got-more-than-what-I-had-ever-dreamt-of-Akshay-Kumar/articleshow/21776783.cms

Singh. I remember going and watching every single wrestling match of Dara Singh fighting King Kong. My father was proud of me throughout, but was most happy when he first saw me on screen… I need him every day.'[46]

Charity Shelters in the Name of His Hero

Akshay has named his production house after his father: Hari Om Entertainment. And now, Akshay has extended his love by starting a cancer shelter, exclusively for police personnel, under his dad's name: Hari Om Cancer Shelter. This, he said, has been a long-standing dream for him.

The idea to start a cancer shelter for policemen came when his father was undergoing chemotherapy at the Tata Memorial hospital. Akshay noticed that many policemen, who came for treatment in the city, would often face trouble with their stay and food arrangements. Now, at his Hari Om Cancer Shelter a policeman undergoing treatment in Mumbai can avail its services of staying in air-conditioned rooms and getting food by paying only ₹400 per day.

---

[46]https://timesofindia.indiatimes.com/entertainment/hindi/bollywood/news/Ive-got-more-than-what-I-had-ever-dreamt-of-Akshay-Kumar/articleshow/21776783.cms

> 'My dad was my best friend and greatest role model. He was an amazing dad, coach, mentor, soldier, husband and friend.'
>
> —*Tiger Woods*

A Martial Arts Pujari

Akshay worships martial arts as he feels it is more than a sport; it is a lifestyle. He says that in China for instance, you don't get a degree before at least two years of training because they are that serious about this sport. It teaches you to fight, but actually cools you down mentally. He says that in Bangkok everyone folds their hands in greeting (much like 'namaste' in India). The greeting is not just for tourists, but they do so in their homes too. It gives one inner calm and confidence, and Akshay feels that countries which practice this have humble and cool-headed citizens.

He first joined martial arts as a child because he was jealous of a boy in his neighbourhood who impressed girls with his martial arts' move, which made Akshay feel humiliated. His father later encouraged him to go to Bangkok to train further in martial arts, but he was expected to support himself by doing some odd jobs as well. He would cook and serve food at a restaurant there while training in Thai boxing and Tai Chi. He is a six-degree black-belt holder (there would be only about fifteen across India).

Jab They Met

Twinkle Khanna started her film career with a Rajkumar Santoshi-directed movie, *Barsaat* (1995). It was the debut for actor Bobby Deol as well. The film turned out to be a moderate hit. Akshay on the other hand started his career with a non-descript role in Mahesh Bhatt's *Aaj* (1987) and received his first major hit in Abbas-Mustan's *Khiladi* (1992).

Twinkle and Akshay first met during a shoot for *Filmfare* magazine in Mumbai, where he developed an instant crush on Twinkle. In one of his interviews with *Filmfare*, the actor confessed, 'I met Twinkle for the first time during a photo session with Jayesh Sheth for *Filmfare*. I still have that photograph. Thank you, *Filmfare*!'[47]

They fell in love during their shooting of the film *International Khiladi* (1999) and decided to take their

---

[47] https://www.filmfare.com/features/i-never-had-to-do-anything-to-impress-twinkle-akshay-kumar-3269.html

relationship further. Since she was the daughter of former superstar, Rajesh Khanna, and a celebrated actress, Dimple Kapadia, Akshay had to be accepted by the family first. And that happened soon enough as Akshay's honesty and charm clicked with them, he came out with flying colours.

On an episode of the popular TV show, *Koffee with Karan*, Akshay revealed that Twinkle was very confident about the success of her film, *Mela*, which was to be released in 2000. She was certain that it would do well and told him that if the movie failed to create magic at the box office, she would marry him. Luckily for both of them, the movie flopped, and soon they got married in 2001.

Again in sync with their choice of remaining grounded, they did not go for a big bash with foreign locales or loud band baja baaraat, but instead went for a simple wedding with just fifty guests at Abu Jani and Sandeep Khosla's residence. No fanfare, but short and sweet—that too in just two hours.

Akshay always gives credit to his wife for bringing peace, love, and stability into his life. He says it was only Twinkle's unfailing support that encouraged him to become a Bollywood star. After the marriage she left her career as an actor and became an interior decorator, an entrepreneur, a bestselling author, a homemaker, a loving and caring mother and a supporting wife—now this is the true definition of a super woman, isn't it? On *Koffee with Karan*, Akshay also talked about the secret behind their strong relationship. He said, 'We keep discovering new things about each other as we are poles apart as individuals.'

The most important thing is to have a supportive wife and that is what a man looks for in his life partner. Balanced, prepared to see the larger picture, and with the attitude that it's 'us' and not 'me' that counts the most. Husband and wife have to support each other in difficult times and stand by each other like a rock. It is these kinds of vows that are taken during marriage rites. But how many couples truly practice what they say at their ceremony?

For Akshay, his wife has been his support system through thick and thin. 'Twinkle has not only added to my wardrobe but also to my bank balance. I was a scattered person; she is the one who has put me together. After marriage, she has kind of raised me (laughs). On a serious note, whenever I've broken-down she's given me emotional support.'[48]

He further substantiates, 'My wife is the best person any man could wish to wake up next to. She holds me up when I'm falling, and puts me down when I'm flying. She makes me

---

[48]https://m.dailyhunt.in/news/india/english/bollywoodshaadis-epaper-bshadi/the+super+romantic+love+story+of+bollywood+s+khiladi+akshay+kumar+and+twinkle+khanna-newsid-81567209

laugh when I'm sad, and moans when I am sitting idle. Tina is everything for me. She is my reality check.'[49]

On his part, Akshay always believed in her and supported her, especially when she decided to switch her career. She said in an interview, 'He really believes in my capabilities as a person and that gave me a lot of confidence to switch jobs. Even today, if I do something new, he ensures he is a part of it. For instance, I have been writing a weekly column in a newspaper since a year now, but he still reads all my pieces before I submit them.'[50]

His Wife Is His Lucky Charm

'The one idea that changed my life was the day I decided to get married to my wife.'

—*Akshay Kumar*[51]

---

[49]https://www.missmalini.com/2016/05/28/tina-everything-akshay-kumar-talks-wife-twinkle-khanna/
[50]https://www.mid-day.com/articles/twinkle-khanna-the-shining-star/15600158
[51]https://www.bollywoodshaadis.com/articles/akshay-kumar-and-twinkle-khanna-love-story-4079

Akshay Kumar thinks of Twinkle as his lucky charm. In an interview he said that he had had fourteen flops in a row and it was only after they got married in 2001 that lady luck smiled at him and things started looking up. For him, his wife is a true 'Lakshmi' who has been very lucky for him. He attributes his stardom, his money, and a stable happy life to his wife.

Before marriage, he had the image of a Casanova and had several alleged link-ups with his co-stars like Raveena Tandon and Shilpa Shetty. But marriage had a sobering effect on him. His sun sign is Virgo; and Virgos are known to work towards a stable and steady life, and are prone to self-analysis and introspection.

Twinkle, being a Capricorn, is hard-working and likes to control things. That is what has brought stability and some routine in his life. They have stood by each other like solid walls and no link-up story—however silly—could ruin their marriage which only grew stronger with the arrival of their son, Aarav, in September, 2002 and daughter, Nitara, in September, 2012, in their lives. No wonder these sun signs have matched and have given a good, happy, and healthy family life to them.

Superstar as Super Parent

Akshay Kumar, besides being a superstar, is also the father of Aarav and Nitara. He takes immense care in making sure he inculcates all the family values in his son, and is protective and supportive towards both kids. Good manners and humility is what he wants his children to learn from him. 'I am proud to be his (Aarav's) father. He has great values and respects elders. That's all I want,' he says while also praising his wife Twinkle Khanna by calling her 'an amazing mom.'[52]

How many children these days actually listen to their parents' advice about living a healthy and organized life? Today, parents try their best to put some sense into their young children but not all of them succeed.

He doesn't like to spoil his children and ensures they do not become arrogant and spendthrift. They travel economy class by air most of the times. Mr Raj Kapoor apparently did something similar with his children. Rishi Kapoor recalls in his autobiography *Khullam Khulla: Rishi Kapoor Uncensored* (2017): 'We were sent to school by public transport because my parents didn't want us to grow up with a sense of

---

[52] http://www.dnaindia.com/entertainment/interview-birthday-special-akshay-kumar-opens-up-about-his-son-aarav-2123353

entitlement.'[53] This is the most intriguing aspect of today's parenting that most parents who have double income have enough surplus money and spoil their children by giving them more than required in terms of money, phones, bikes, and even cars, and let them splurge. We are yet to learn that children need to be made to understand the value of money and not be careless about it. We ape the West when it comes to most things, but seldom learn good things like punctuality, dignity of labour, being polite to others and even spending within your means, from them.

Akshay Kumar, however, is clear that whatever his kids will get, they will have to earn every bit of it, and thus he wants his children to learn to earn. 'So, we decided to go on a family holiday and Aarav would travel business class. He is getting to travel business class because he worked hard to get his first degree black belt (in kudo). If he hadn't got it, he would have travelled economy. He has travelled economy on many occasions without cribbing because he understands that he needs to earn it, nothing is handed to him on a platter.'[54]

---

[53]Iyer, Meena and Kapoor, Rishi, *Khullam Khulla: Rishi Kapoor Uncensored*, HarperCollins India, 2017.
[54]https://www.hindustantimes.com/bollywood/nothing-is-handed-to-my-kids-on-a-platter-they-have-to-earn-it-akshay-kumar/story-3MjXxXWiFsCHcGlTG85LUL.html

'I want them to be responsible human beings who are also full of gratitude for what they have. *Kuch khairat mein nahi milta*, (you don't inherit everything) whatever they get is achieved by them...,' Akshay says.[55] To make him self-reliant, he sent his son Aarav to the UK at the age of thirteen for a self-reliance training camp. Now that's parenting done right!

'It is not what you do for your children, but what you taught them to do for themselves, that will make them successful human beings.'

—*Ann Landers*

Giving Your Kids the Right 'Sanskars'

As I always say, 'Sanskars can be given by parents but they also have to be taken by the children'. If Akshay's dad has given him these good habits, the former too is worthy of praise for having actually followed them. He lived like an ordinary young boy brought up with meagre means but good values

---

[55] http://www.dnaindia.com/entertainment/interview-birthday-special-akshay-kumar-opens-up-about-his-son-aarav-2123353

by his parents. And it reflects even today in his dealings with people, his professional ethics, and the way he is bringing up his own children.

Unfortunately the rich and the mighty in India—most of them—do not play a positive role in the upbringing of their children. They think they are the kings but don't behave like kings. Most of them pamper them and are responsible for creating the inflated egos of their own children. *'Tu janta hai mera baap kaun hai?'* has not come out of thin air. Here the 'baap' (father) is more responsible for his child's stupid and irresponsible behaviour. I always tell the parents of my students that they are the ones who have to keep their children in check. Parents are role models and children just follow what their parents do. Our society has taken a beating and we are in a crisis mode today with juvenile crime rate shooting through the ceiling because today's parents do not control their children as our parents did. Parents shouldn't outsource their responsibilities.

Akshay Kumar comes as a whiff of fresh air in such times; he may be a doting father but he teaches his children charity and good behaviour. And as they say, charity begins at home; his son, Aarav, and he often clean up their cupboards themselves and whatever is not needed is neatly packed and given to an orphanage where the young boy himself goes to give these things personally. How many rich brats, if I may say so, do this? I feel it is not *what* charity is done but *how* charity is done—that is more important for character-building. There are very few parents who do that today.

Home Is Where the Heart Is

'Where are we really going? Always home!'

—Novalis

One needs the emotional attachment that comes with homes and not the synthetic feeling of living in a hotel. That is the basic difference between a home and a house. Akshay and Twinkle have an unrestricted view of the Arabian Sea from their Juhu home. For Twinkle, every home that she's lived in has always had a mango tree. The home she lived in till she was twelve, the iconic 'Aashirwad' on Mumbai's Carter Road, had a mango tree growing outside the dining area. She now has a sea-facing duplex apartment with her husband and kids, and it also has a mango tree. Fond of reading and writing, she has created a cosy library in the apartment to store her crates of books under the staircase which people use for either shoes or as a storage dump.

Also, it is always good to have your family and friends close by. Most people may not be able to afford this but many who can also never bother to ensure this. Twinkle and Akshay are very thoughtful and they have his sister and mother stay in the same building. Even her business partner, who is also a close friend, stays in the same complex. Living enveloped by their friends and family is important to the couple.[56] This is probably the sentiments behind the phrase: 'Home sweet home'.

Family Man: Work-Life Balance

Part of the Kumar persona is his clear work-life balance. Kumar works strictly eight hours a day and takes Sundays off to spend time with his wife, son, and daughter. On Saturdays he works from 7 to 2 p.m., so that he gets rest of the Saturday free. His wife Twinkle decided to switch from acting to interior designing and is now also a bestselling author. I feel this is the best way to achieve work-life balance when both husband

---

[56]https://www.vogue.in/content/celebrity-homes-twinkle-khanna-and-akshay-kumars-artful-mumbai-abode

and wife decide their parental responsibilities and accordingly define their priorities in life. Had she continued with films, they would have had little time for themselves as well as their children. These are the most important decisions of life and at the end of the day these make the most difference in leading a happy one.

'A man travels the world over in search of what he needs and returns home to find it.'

—George A. Moore

What can you learn from Akshay Kumar about family and happiness?

1. Respect and love for parents and elders comes first in life.
2. One must make efforts to have a balance between work and personal life. However busy or great you may be, with some effort it is always possible.
3. Invest in your home in terms of comfort and style. Do your best to make your living space cosy and comfortable. After all that is the place you go to after a day's work.

4. Accord respect and priority to your family and even extended family because they are the ones who will always stand by you and will support you unconditionally.
5. Sometimes, a simple thing like going for a walk with your loved ones is more important than a ton of money.
6. You are lucky to have parents and have their blessings. So, make use of their good wishes, because many people are not lucky enough to have that privilege.